GOLF
How Good
Do You
Want to Be?

GOLF
How Good Do You Want to Be?

Dr. Bill Kroen

**Andrews McMeel
Publishing**
Kansas City

04 05 06 07 08 MLT 10 9 8 7 6 5 4 3 2 1

Library of Congress Cataloging-in-Publication Data

Kroen, William C.
Golf : how good do you want to be? / by Bill Kroen.
p. cm.
ISBN: 0-7407-4193-4
1. Golf. 2. Golf—Psychological aspects. I. Title.
GV965.K735   2004
796.352—dc22   2003070861

Book design and composition by
Kelly & Company, Lee's Summit, Missouri

ATTENTION: SCHOOLS AND BUSINESSES

Andrews McMeel books are available at quantity discounts with bulk purchase for educational, business, or sales promotional use. For information, please write to: Special Sales Department, Andrews McMeel Publishing, 4520 Main Street, Kansas City, Missouri 64111.

To my family,

Kathy, Kerry, and Kristen,

with love and gratitude

Contents

Foreword

"How good do you want to be?" is certainly a great question for golfers. I love the title of this book and I am confident that the book will help your game tremendously. My good friend Bill Kroen has given us a wonderful, insightful, and refreshing approach to this very complex game of golf. His book is a must for anyone serious about getting to the next level in his or her golf game.

I first met Bill in 2003 at Fore Seasons Golf and Learning Center in Hingham, Massachusetts, where I have been conducting all-women golf schools for two seasons. I was flattered when he asked me to give him a lesson. On the range he started booming drives out over 250 yards, so I looked up and simply said, "We'd better go to the putting green." It was clearly evident that Bill was very knowledgeable about all aspects of the game and that he possesses a wonderful golf swing. It was like watching a clinic.

Golf: How Good Do You Want to Be? is written for golfers of all levels. It covers golf to the fullest by explaining all the aspects of the game. Dr. Bill's background in psychology and golf enables him to present a comprehensive approach that combines the physical, motivational, and mental elements of the game in a manner that is eminently understandable. I wish this book had been written sooner!

Sandra Palmer, LPGA
1975 U.S. Women's Open champion

Acknowledgments

It is such a wonderful situation in life to be involved with the game of golf. The greatest aspect, I feel, is the people associated with the game in one way or another. This book has been greatly enhanced by these people to whom I owe a sincere thank-you for their help: the U.S. Open champion Sandra Palmer, who has been my instructor and friend; Dr. Arnold Scheller, a skilled and renowned surgeon who enabled me to remain playing the game that I love; and Dr. Chris Olivieri, who has enabled me to strive to play my best through strength and flexibility and who has taught me so much about how our muscles work.

Thanks are also in order to PGA professionals Mike McBroom and Toby Lyons, as well as Ed Antonelli, Bill Carnes, Matt Wilson, and John Leahy for their advice and counsel. A special thank-you to my agent, Andy Zack, whose knowledge, diligence, and hard work have been invaluable to me through the years. I am very grateful to have Dorothy O'Brien as an editor. Most of all, I wish to thank my wife, Kathy, for her love and encouragement.

Introduction

The question "How good do you want to be?" is one that I hope you will pause and reflect on as you look at your golfing life. The answer depends on how much commitment and value you place on becoming the best golfer that you can be. You must weigh how important golf is to you.

Is it a once-a-week or once-a-month afternoon recreation or is it your avocation? Is the game of golf more than a game to you? Is golf a source of recreation, exhilaration, challenge, and fascination? If you answered in the affirmative to the last two questions then you are ready to accept change, play better, and realize that the hours you spend playing the game of golf should be fun and rewarding to you.

When you ask yourself, "Why do I play golf?" it is always better if your answers are positive: that you play for enjoyment, for the joy of being outdoors with friends and family, and for the exhilaration of doing well at something that you enjoy. This book is about and for people who really love golf—who want to play better and who want to learn as a process. The learning process is and has to be part of the journey of enjoying the game. Practice, gaining awareness, reading, observing, and absorbing little insights and exploring the wonders of the game are all the fun parts of the game and not just hurdles in the way of getting somewhere. As you set out on the road to becoming a better player, start from a standpoint of building and developing as a child would build and develop through the primary years of development. Drink in the environment and culture of golf, from knowledge of the swing to the rich history that makes the game so fascinating. Don't *struggle* to learn—*love* to learn.

In researching this book, I looked at handicaps at my club from ten years ago and compared them to current ones. There is almost no difference for the vast majority of players. In other words, most adult golfers reach a level and then stay at that level for their golfing lives. I tried to analyze the reasons for this, and this question became the basis for this book. Staying at a level of play for a lifetime may be acceptable for many, and actually it is a source of comfort for us as humans. Still, it is somewhat surprising that despite years of additional practice and experience and revolutionary gains in the technology of equipment, few golfers actually improve.

Why exactly is it hard to improve? One of the major obstacles to making a change in almost anything we do is the nature of change itself. In the late 1930's the medical community acknowledged the phenomenon of homeostasis. Homeostasis is the body's way of regulating itself and resisting change in order to remain normal in all of its functions. If we become too hot, our bodies secrete sweat to cool our skin and slow our heart rate and muscle activity. If you sprain an ankle, your body sends blood to swell the area to prevent movement while it heals and sends pain signals to prevent its use. These are two simple examples in a myriad of complex functions that our brains do every day to regulate our bodies. Scientists are still discovering how the brain works its miracles.

Another aspect of homeostasis is that we have a built-in predisposition to avoid change. Not only do our bodies spring into action to restore health when a virus enters them, but our minds react when any change is brought into our known environment. Homeostatic behavior even extends to organizations. Corporations have learned that in order to make significant change they must bring in outside help and advice to execute the change. So what does all this mean to the golfer?

As I looked at how the vast majority of golfers made little or no improvement, I also took a look at those who did make dramatic gains. The two groups that made change for the better were young people or beginners and a group of individuals who took on a program of golf development. Young people make changes much more easily than adults. They are in a learning mode. They expect and welcome change in their lives. Languages, mathematics, and even values and opinions are developed without major resistance. Learning the golf swing and concepts of the game come as fresh ideas and feelings and not a foreign invader that upsets their homeostasis. Learn from self-awareness and feel you are well ahead of the game in seeking improvement. Let go of any worries about taming that slice or about what other people might think of you as you play or practice. Let yourself become free to learn and allow that freedom to give you the gift of acceptance to change and the peaceful confidence that will always hold the promise of better things to come in your golf game.

Those who made dramatic changes not only in golf but also in other sports and life itself all had several things in common. They were willing to accept change. They knew that staying in the present mode, no matter what it was, was no longer acceptable to them. They realized that they needed to become active learners, to admit that they needed to make a change, and to acknowledge that the change may be difficult, but they were willing to give it a go in order to get what they want or needed in golf, sports, or life. I spoke to many top professionals and to amateurs who play the game at the top levels of competition. I have spoken with and read about professionals in other sports who have achieved greatness as well as everyday people who have made major changes in their games and lives. *Golf: How Good Do You Want to Be?* is a reflection of my research and training as both a mental health and golf professional.

Improving your golf game significantly is not a matter of drudgery or wearing a hair shirt. It does not come to an end with a certain result. Instead, improving your golf game is a rewarding, fun, and enlightening process that will transcend how you go about becoming a better player to how you view life as well. I do not mean to sound mystical, but once you set a plan or process in motion to become better, you cannot but help becoming better in other things that you do as well. By learning how to change, restructuring your thinking, and learning to strategize you are gaining tools that become collateral assets in your makeup and make you better at whatever you do.

I have had students go from hopeless players to club champions. I have had a student go from being an average player with good promise to becoming a state champion. It can and does happen. My only suggestion is to place yourself in a learning mode like a child and be willing to accept change knowing that you will become better beyond your greatest expectations. My only requirement is that you allow yourself to be free of fear of failing or of a sense of impending doom when you are playing. Bring a fresh and open mind filled with realistic but positive expectations that you can and will become a much better golfer; get out of your own way and take a fresh perspective, of learning for the love of the game itself. The results that you want will follow. Let's begin enjoying and learning the process of loving golf and becoming a better golfer.

CHAPTER ONE

The Mind-Body Connection

NO OTHER SPORT FUSES THE MIND AND BODY AS MUCH AS GOLF. FOOTBALL, baseball, and tennis are sports in which we react to a moving ball and the reactions are reflexive in nature. The pitcher fires a fastball and the hitter reacts while his subconscious mind calculates the speed and location of the ball and helps him to swing on a plane that will meet it. If asked to calculate the physics behind this moment in the game, no major-leaguer would be able to offer a formula. Yogi Berra once said, "You can't hit and think at the same time."

Yogi was absolutely on the money and well ahead of the sports psychologists who followed decades later after his observation. If, while driving to work, you had to consciously think of positioning your hands on the wheel to make a turn, gauging your speed, and moving your foot from accelerator to brake, you would be in an accident in no time. You have to trust your brain and subconscious mind to perform the needed tasks without your conscious brain's "interference." It's the same in golf: the more we try to control things the more we lose control. The brain, while the greatest and most intricate of all computers ever designed, can only handle a few tasks at one time. Performing a physical movement while trying to direct that movement through conscious thought is practically impossible.

I often spend hours on practice ranges and take breaks to watch others hit balls. Golfers seldom speak to others on the range, but they wear their emotions on their sleeves. You often see a golfer who pauses between shots and has a grim, determined look on his face as if he is trying to overcome an insurmountable task that life has thrown in front of him. There is little joy but mostly frustration, anger, and deep despair between attempts to hit a golf ball correctly. Recently, in Florida, I watched a man come to the range at the exact same time every day. He would spend almost two hours per day hitting balls mostly in total frustration. Every so often he would hit a good shot and hold his pose and watch it well after it had stopped rolling. Yet in the long run, these practice sessions only led to feelings of inadequacy and defeat.

I saw this man agonize over his shots day after day and wondered what his goal was in golf. I wondered whether he had a goal at all. He may have equated hitting hundreds and thousands of balls with making improvement. I did notice that he never made any changes in his swing, made a pre-shot routine, or stopped to align himself and connect to a target. He simply machine-gunned his shots one after the other. My wife suggested that I go over and help him. I declined because a golfer or anyone wanting to make something better in his life must truly want to change. This man was not taking lessons or asking for help. Maybe he was content beating balls every day as a means of exercise.

At every range there is a diverse group of golfers. There is the guy who only blasts drivers as far as he can. These guys usually have a girlfriend to impress watching from behind and will swing with a vicious motion that sends the ball long and wild. There is the thinker who is perpetually tinkering with his grip, stance, posture, swing plane, and anything else he or she can manipulate. Each shot brings a new wrinkle in the swing with the hope that it will produce the key to golf nirvana. Some players slam their clubs in anger after each shot; some talk out loud, calling either themselves or the ball names; some offer themselves instruction such as, "Slow it down, you idiot!"

It is very unlikely that any of the above players will realize any significant improvement in their golf games and in their enjoyment of the game itself. One basic of the mind is that we tend to gravitate toward things that are pleasurable to us and avoid unpleasant, dangerous, or uncomfortable things. This is blatantly obvious to us, so why do golfers continue to subject themselves to self-hate, anger, and frustration on a regular basis? The National Golf Foundation reports that 25 to 30 percent of golfers leave the game each year, only to be replaced by about the same number of beginners.

On the other hand, there are often youngsters hitting balls on the range as well. They laugh with delight when the ball flies into the air. Their swings are free and there is never anger and frustration. They are having fun and hitting shots that delight them. I often help a youngster with a little pointer to assist them with balance or help them place their hands on the club in a better way. They are thankful for the help and, more important, make the change almost immediately with good results. For years, I taught inner-city kids golf each spring. The local PGA pro, Bob Carey, would give me clubs for the kids and for most of them it was the first time they ever had seen or held a golf club. I would show them a few basics and then have them watch me swing and hit balls. Every year I was surprised at how well they mimicked my swing and how well they learned and progressed. They hit the balls with joy and I loved to see them finish like Tiger Woods as the ball shot down range. Some of them went on to play in high school and college and many enjoy golf on a regular basis as young adults. That I was able to introduce them to the game and help them down the road to becoming good golfers has brought me a great sense of pride. They taught me as well: how, if you are in a learning mode, you make great gains and master the fundamentals of golf in a short period.

The Color of Golf

So much of what we do in all aspects of our lives is dependant on our perspective and attitude toward the people, places, and things that we encounter. We can choose the state of mind or awareness that we want to live in. We have it within us to be happy, peaceful, and thoughtful people. We know through the study of the mind that the highest-functioning people are those who have extraordinary awareness of their environment. They are truly caring about other people, unselfish, and accomplished at what they do because it is important to them, and they are aware of where they are and what is going on in their world. The last part might seem a little obvious to you. Aware of where they are?

How many times have you been in traffic that is completely stalled? Look around and you will see people who are cursing and sounding their horns as if that will correct the problem. Is that person really aware of where he is? Does he know that the traffic is jammed and might be that way for a reason that is completely out of his control? Does he really think that by sounding his horn and swearing he will make people open a path for him, or somewhere in the distance people will hear his horn and snap to correcting the traffic problem at a rapid pace? Such a person really does not know where he is. I might have felt this way at times in the past but now I take the opportunity of a traffic jam to look at things such as buildings and landscape that I would have never seen before, going by at 60 miles per hour.

The color of the man's mind who is blowing his horn in vain is red—the color of anger. His brain is firing negative chemicals that will speed his heart rate, raise his blood pressure, tense his muscles, and place him in a self-defeating mood that may transfer to other aspects in his day ahead. The color of golf is green. It is peaceful, refreshing, and calming and represents renewal and life itself. It allows us to go at a stop light, frames the color of flowers and presents a miniature piece of art when a white ball lies on top of the grass. When you step onto a golf course or practice range from this day forward, I want you to place yourself into a green mode. Sense the calmness, freedom, joy, and sense of renewal from the green that surrounds you. You are now becoming aware of where you are and you are part of the environment and not an alien visitor. Your awareness now sets the framework for both learning and enjoyment. Your mind is calm and free and ready to accept change and play golf from a standpoint of children having fun as they make leaps in their learning.

Golf is such a beautiful game. In what other sport do we come so close to nature? We smell the grass, watch the birds, and marvel at trees, ponds, and streams. Every hole is different, every shot a new challenge, every day a new beginning. How did so many get so frustrated and angry that they would quit the game and walk away from the beauty and joy that the game offers all of us? I feel that somewhere along the line, the golfer who gave up never gave himself the chance to become good at the game so that the golf experience was pleasurable and rewarding, not drudgery.

A friend of mine was such a golfer. He played every day, rain or shine. He would play well in spurts and occasionally have a good round. Most of the time, however, his golf experience was one of agony and depression. He spent almost all of his time on the course complaining and feeling down about his game. One time on a tee, he stood in the address position for what seemed to be an eternity. Finally, he looked up to the rest of us and said, "I forgot what to do with my legs." That little episode told it all. His mind had been trying to take complete control of his golf game and he could not let it go. He could not just play the game nor could he let himself enjoy it. It is important to remember that we need to get out of our own way at times and let things happen. Within a year my friend sold his clubs and left the game as it was a source of negativity in his life.

In his book *Golf for Enlightenment*, Deepak Chopra tells us to promise "not to struggle." This bit of wisdom carries a great deal of truth and meaning for playing the game of golf and living our lives. We often struggle unnecessarily. In golf, we let one bad hole define us as a bad golfer or let it ruin the rest of the round as we let anger or frustration become our dominant feeling. I think we should invoke the Fifth Amendment in golf. We should say to ourselves, " I refuse to let that double bogey bother me—otherwise it will tend to ruin the rest of my day." Our day can be filled with struggle if we let traffic, for example, make us irritable and angry and set us off for the day. We can let others push our buttons and let ourselves become less productive or more unhappy because of resentment. Deepak Chopra was so right in telling us to keep a promise to ourselves not to make things difficult. Let the swing happen and let the traffic take care of itself. Feeling angry and frustrated will not bring about change.

Chopra's thought came to me recently while I was playing in a tournament. I was cruising around well on a day that was pouring rain with a cold, raw wind. On a par-4 hole I hit a good drive but came up short in heavy, wet rough on my second shot. I tried to hit a wedge up and out on the rough but the ball only went a few feet. I got the ball onto the green, then three-putted for a double bogey. My first reaction was to feel frustrated and my thoughts turned to how I was blowing any chance of doing well in the tournament. Then, I did some slow breathing, made a little smile to myself, and promised not to struggle. The scoring was going to be high that day and I went to the next hole with a renewed feeling of calmness and confidence. I went on to play well and finished second. The message for me was that I could not change the past so I would not let it control my future. It not only makes sense but is also a healthy means to improving the outcome of what we face.

I believe that all of us are capable of making significant change once we learn how to do it. We can play at a level that that will bring us enjoyment and satisfaction so that golf becomes a joyful part of our recreation time and enriches our lives in general. We need to concentrate on process or the journey rather than results. We can and should set realistic goals but whether your goal is to lower your handicap by five strokes or play professionally, you need to focus on the daily process of improving and, more important, on changing.

The Learning Scheme

Education experts have identified three types of learning: *cognitive,* a body of collected knowledge; *affective,* by means of attitudes, motivation, and appreciation; and *psychomotor,* the combination of mind and body that builds and acquires skills. As we move through this book, emphasis will be placed on all three types of learning. To learn the game properly, all three must be used.

Getting Out of Your Own Way

If positive change is going to occur, we need to let it happen in a planned, orderly method where we let ourselves improve by accepting change and letting go of the control that we think we have. If your golf swing is not producing good golf shots, you are going to have to make some changes. These changes will feel foreign and you will naturally try to resist them. To begin your journey to becoming a good golfer the first promise you must make to yourself is to accept change and not fight. Be like a child by placing yourself in a learning mode, ready to absorb all that is offered, willing to copy and change both mentally and physically how you approach your golf game.

In golf, a teaching pro will often tell a student to get out of his or her own way, meaning to clear or open the hips through impact to allow the club to swing freely toward the target. If we did not clear our hips out of the way, we would make a stiff pass at the ball with our arms only. In the same way, thoughts like "What am I supposed to do with my legs?" are "control" thoughts that also block the free swing that is within us. The feeling of a golf swing is one of lightness and freedom. Thoughts that are designed to control our movements consciously are ones that promote tension and restriction. As you learn the correct method of making a good golf swing, simply incorporate it into your subconscious and let the swing happen. Accept the changes and turn it over to your inner self. Many top touring professionals speak of having no conscious thought of hitting at the ball when they swing.

We have all had moments or even periods when every shot we hit was great or when it seemed that every putt went in. Professionals often refer to this as being "in the zone." At these times there is no conscious thought of what we are doing. We simply swing or stroke the putt and everything seems to go our way. We are in a state where we are not thinking or trying but simply letting it happen. I remember watching a Chicago Bulls game where Michael Jordan came down-court and launched six consecutive three-point shots that hit nothing but net. After the sixth one, he turned toward his bench and lifted his arms as if to say, "I don't know what is going on!" He was in the zone and just letting it take him along for the ride. In Tiger Woods's last U.S. Amateur Championship he made long putt after long putt to stage an incredible comeback. It seemed almost impossible that one man could make putt after putt perfectly under such pressure. Again, he was letting go of the tendency to control the situation. His concentration, focus, and commitment were high, but he simply turned the execution over to his natural ability.

It is interesting to note how major changes in getting over difficult things can occur through letting go and getting out of our own way. One of the most difficult things to change and recover from is alcohol or drug addiction. Most therapies fail miserably and many medical experts feel helpless in the face of people who are caught in addiction. Johns Hopkins University did a study of all the therapeutic methods used to treat addiction to find which ones were effective. Only one had a remarkable success rate, that used by Alcoholics Anonymous. The study tried to analyze why but could not quantify exactly why over 80 percent of hopeless alcoholics succeeded in AA's program while they failed miserably in some of the best medical therapies and hospitals. One component that distinguishes AA from other treatments is that in AA, alcoholics are advised to let go of trying to control their drinking, their lives, and the lives of others. They are told to turn it over to a higher power and let their recovery happen. This getting out of the way has proved effective. The less we try to consciously control things the more we gain freedom to learn and improve. The lesson for golfers is clear. Let go and learn to become better.

The Winning Attitude

Psychologist have long understood the dynamic of the self-fulfilling prophecy. People who feel that they cannot succeed or are doomed to fail are more likely to fail at what they are attempting despite their best efforts. The onetime heavyweight champion Floyd Patterson had fought his way to the top defeating opponents who were bigger and more powerful than he was. In 1962, he had a title fight against Sonny Liston against the advice of his manager, Cus D'Amato. D'Amato told Patterson that he could never beat Liston. Patterson became convinced that he was going to lose, to the point that he brought a disguise—a beard and a fake nose—to wear out of the auditorium after he was beaten by Liston. Patterson was knocked out in the first round.

In golf, a winning, confident attitude is almost essential to playing well. This attitude is not one of bragging or trying to show people up. It is an inner confidence that comes from practice, knowing the mechanics, trusting your swing, eliminating negatives in the mind, and blocking out anything that comes between you and good golf. The very best players all have a manner about them of quiet confidence. They even walk in an athletic rhythm down the fairway, head up, shoulders square, with a long determined stride. I have often told my students to "walk like a champion."

Norman Vincent Peale, in his book *Positive Thinking Every Day: An Inspiration for Each Day of the Year,* wrote, "People become really remarkable when they start thinking that they can do things. When they believe in themselves, they have discovered the first secret of success." You have great possibilities within you. Allow yourself to reach those possibilities by seeing your potential and then going after it. In golf, take pride in your improvement and recognize that you are in a process that is life-long. The goals that you set may be attained but you will always be a life-long learner and life-long player.

In high school I played baseball on a team one of whose members became a star in the major leagues. A friend once said that he thought this player was "cocky." It wasn't cockiness that made him stand out above the rest of us, it was a level of confidence and belief in his own abilities that took him on his journey up the ladder to the top. It was his self-esteem and trust, which allowed his body to execute the physical parts of fielding and hitting a baseball. His mind was the tool that both produced and allowed his greatness to happen. When you are around PGA touring professionals or major-league players, you will notice that they have an aura about them that comes from having experienced that special feeling of total self-confidence and trust in themselves to perform.

Our motivation to become good at what we do is an integral part of the human condition. In the early stages in the study of psychology, researchers believed that the primary human motivational goal was to eliminate stimulation and to be in a state of calm with nothing to prod us too far from status quo as that would cause a disruption in our state. The twentieth-century American psychologist Abraham Maslow changed our views as to what motivates us in life both consciously and subconsciously. Maslow's hierarchy of needs that must be fulfilled in man does in fact relate in the upper levels to our inner desires to excel at something, including golf.

Maslow's pyramid of motives, from the bottom to the top, is as follows:

1. Physiological—all humans are motivated to survive and seek food, shelter, and warmth.
2. Security and safety.
3. Love and a feeling of belonging.
4. Competence, prestige, and self-esteem.
5. Self-actualization.

Levels 3 to 5 all have relevance to our desire to become good at something such as golf. Becoming very proficient at the game can be spurred by our inner desire to be appreciated and be desirable company. We work at our game to display competence, earn prestige, and, more important, feel good about ourselves and fulfill ourselves through attaining our goals. As golf is a game that can never be fully mastered, it is an ongoing search for improvement through learning. Our curiosity leads us to explore more and more the mysteries of all aspects of the game for greater enjoyment and greater fulfillment.

It is interesting to note the contrast in thinking between great golfers and poor ones. I have asked touring professionals what they think about before and during a shot. The reply is almost always the same. Before the shot they visualize what the shot will look like and how it will feel as they swing. As they approach the ball, they zero in on the target. During the swing, they say they think of nothing. The struggling amateur will first identify all the problems—bunkers, water, out of bounds, deep rough—and focus on them. Once over the ball, the high handicapper gives him- or herself a list of dos and don'ts such as "Straight left arm, keep your head down, don't hit it into the water." When you see a player reach for an old ball on a shot before a water hazard, you know that he is going to hit the ball into the water.

I have watched the top blind golfers in the United States play. I watched the national champion, Joe Lazzaro, play eighteen holes and marvel at how well he could hit the ball and score into the high 70s on difficult courses. Blind golfers are guided by caddies who line them up and give them information on the upcoming shot. I read once that the caddies will not mention water hazards, out of bounds, or other trouble to their players, as this will eliminate any source of worry from them as they play the shot. We can learn from them that being blind to trouble can actually free us to shift our focus to the target. It is not so much that we are tricking our mind as that we are using it more productively. You do not have to be brilliant to be a good golfer but you do need to know how to think and how to focus.

The frame of mind that we are in for the day has a major role in how we play. Byron Nelson once said that in order to have a slow rhythm for the day, he would even shave slowly. Many players listen to a song over and over on the way to the course and then carry that song in their heads throughout the round, often humming it to themselves. Others like to have one thought, such as "smooth," as they set up to the ball.

In practice swing, thoughts such as, "Keep the club low and slow on the take-away" serve as a link between the mind and body to promote a connection and refine a skill. The best advice from the best players is never to hit a shot without a focus of some kind.

A winning attitude comes from many areas within us. Good shots promote our self-confidence and tell us that we have the potential to play well if only we could harness the positive things that we did in that swing. The trick here is to do the things that will instill that attitude. It will not just appear in a flash of enlightenment. We have to recognize it as a goal and work at developing it every day in our golfing lives.

One key to creating a positive attitude is how we view ourselves and how we talk to ourselves. In working with young children with low self-esteem, I would insist that they would use only self-affirmations when they spoke of themselves. When they said negative things about themselves, I would ignore or redirect them. When they spoke in positives, I would praise and reinforce them.

No matter how you play golf, take a look at the successful things that you have accomplished in your life. It could be family, your occupation, music, a hobby, or any achivment that you can take pride in. That ability to be successful and master something is the intangible ingredient that will enable you to become a good or great golfer as well. The fact that you are reading this book is proof that you have a will to change and are taking the steps to make improvement in your game. You are already way ahead of most golfers on the road to playing well. Trust yourself to be successful and see yourself as being a good player.

Golf may be just one aspect of your life. You may have found it as a special gift or talent that you have and want to develop to the highest level of your ability. Josh Hinds writes to an Internet mailing list entitled "Inspiration a Day." He has written: "Whether or not we realize it, each of us has a special gift just waiting to surface! . . . We are developing these gifts not only for ourselves but those around us as well. . . . The important thing here is not what your gift is as much as that you develop it so you can share it with those around you and in the process further your own personal life."

To excel at golf is not as altruistic as finding a cure for a disease, but if that is your gift and calling you make yourself a better person and are able to help others learn to excel through your example at succeeding in one area in life.

I recently had eye surgery and the two surgeons working on me asked if I thought it was possible for them to become good golfers. I joked that I wasn't sure if I would want a surgeon with a one handicap but then went on to answer their question. I pointed out that both men had achieved notable success in a difficult and demanding profession, that they had displayed the discipline and determination to endure rigorous training and demanding requirements, that they possessed eye-hand coordination far beyond most people in the world, and that they were highly intelligent and able to learn. They looked at me without answering, smiled subtly and went on about their business. I hope I planted a little seed of self-discovery and reality for these doctors to know that each of us has the ability to become better at whatever we choose using the success modes that have helped us in our lives.

Remember that one bad shot or one bad hole does not define you as a bad golfer. Many times after a poor hole, a golfer will revert to poor habits as if the bad hole only confirmed what he already knew— that he was a poor player or just didn't have it that day. Even touring professionals are not exempt from this phenomenon. How many times have you watched a professional player who is in contention take a double bogey and then gradually self-destruct on the following holes to play himself out of the tournament? Touring pros refer to this as "throwing up on your shoes," "having a train wreck," or "having the wheels come off the wagon."

On the other hand, I clearly remember an event that has stayed with me longer than any other shot or play in the Masters or U.S. Open. It was years ago when Jack Nicklaus was playing in the San Diego Open at Torrey Pines. As he came to the back nine on the last day he had a narrow lead. With five holes to go, he made a quadruple-bogey 8 on a par-4. Most of us mortals would have folded our tents right then and there. The mind of a champion is different, however. Nicklaus went on to birdie three out of the last four holes and go on to win the tournament. Sure there was talent involved, but that kind of performance separated Jack Nicklaus from the pack of talented touring professionals who were chasing him. He has the mind of a champion.

The technique to manage my emotions that I teach is a one-minute meditation to start afresh. After hitting a bad shot or having a bad hole, I refuse to let that incident become my persona for the rest of the round. Anger, frustration, regret, and worry are useless emotions and will only hurt your chances to play well. After a bad hole I take a quiet moment by myself. I deep-breathe so that my stomach goes out on the inhale and flattens on the exhale. As I make a slow exhale, I feel the tension and negative emotions flow out with my breath. On the inhale, I feel new energy enter my mind and body. One good thing about having a bad hole is that you lose the honors and will have some extra time to perform your calming and reenergizing meditation moment. As I step up to the next shot, I have not forgotten the past as that would be unrealistic, but I feel that the rest of the round is just beginning and that I am free of any negative effects that the past hole might have on me.

In my golfing career I can think of two times when my emotions dictated how I would play for better or worse. The first came when, as a young first lieutenant, I played in the All-Marine Tournament at Camp Pendleton, California. It was my first tournament that had national significance, as the top six players went to the All-Service Tournament to compete against such players as Orville Moody and Homero Blancas. I came to the 16th hole playing well but I had no idea where I stood in relation to the rest of the field. There was a gallery of about a hundred people watching the play at that hole. My drive was in light rough with a clear shot of about 150 yards to the hole. While I was waiting to play, a man from the gallery came over to me and said that if I parred in, I would win the tournament. I remember becoming immediately nervous and my first reaction was to look over at the par-3 17th hole to see where the pin was and what the wind was doing. I hit my shot onto the green and made two putts for a par. On the 17th, I hit my shot about 15 feet from the hole and proceeded to hit my first putt about 8 feet beyond it. I three-putted for a bogey. On the 18th hole, I hit my ball into a fairway bunker despite having a large landing area. I made another bogey to finish third. I made the team but learned how my emotions could take me out of the now and destroy clear thinking and my golf swing.

Recently I was playing in a two-day senior tournament and was among the leaders after the first day. The second day was cold and windy and there was a drenching rain.

Despite the miserable conditions, I plodded along, playing well and staying in contention. On the 13th hole, I hit my second shot into heavy wet rough and ended up with a double bogey. At first I felt any chance of finishing well had disappeared, but then I stood on the next tee and went through my one-minute meditation to reenergize myself. I felt strong again and free of anger or frustration. Despite the worsening storm and impossible conditions, I went on to par four of the last five holes and finished second. It was a quiet victory for me as I won over my emotions although I did not win the tournament. I felt that I had grown as a player.

This little one-minute meditation is not something mystical from Eastern spiritualism. It is based on common medical and psychological principles. If we become nervous and upset, our natural response is to breathe in a quick shallow manner, our muscles tighten, and our brain creates a surge of chemicals that make us operate and think instinctively fast. It is simply the fight-or-flight response that even shows up on the golf course because our brains do not distinguish the source of the fear or doubt that is hitting us. By breathing deeply, we oxygenate our brains and muscles. The brain needs the oxygen to perform normally, not in an automatic panic mode. Our muscles need the oxygen that flows in with the blood to make them operate naturally and fluidly. Our self-talk removes the negative thoughts that are contained in the chemicals being transmitted in our minds. We have renewed our minds and bodies to allow us to play our best in a short period of recovery.

Self-Talk

Most people think in words rather than pictures. Talking to one's self is healthy and essential to executing difficult tasks such as hitting a golf ball. Some golf professionals use what are called "swing thoughts" to cue a movement. It is best to have only one swing thought for the day. Having many thoughts will only overload the circuits and make you freeze over the shot. Swing thoughts must not be too mechanical or technical in nature. For example, you should not say something like "Turn your shoulders forty percent more than your hips." This is a swing stopper and you just can't do it. A better swing thought would be "Get the left shoulder behind the chin." This swing thought is easy to execute and makes a mind-body connection to help you make a full shoulder turn when making your backswing. Later on in the section on practice, we will offer more swing thoughts to help build the mind-body connection.

Swing thoughts that produce good results should be kept in your repertoire. Use them in practice and on the course as a steady, consistent way of making self-talk a productive means of becoming a good golfer. You can get good swing thoughts from reading golf magazines or finding tips on the Internet or anywhere instruction is given. Search around for a simple, affirmative statement that will serve as a reminder to make a certain move that will improve your swing and make you more consistent. Later in this book, we will have swing thoughts and affirmative thinking as we work through the golf shots and course strategy.

Possession of a focused, active mind on the golf course often means the difference between average and good players. You do not need to grind and analyze everything as you play, as that would take the fun out of the game. Being at a higher level of alertness and being able to both calm and stimulate your mind as needed is the delicate balance that we are working to attain. After a round, you should feel that you are somewhat mentally tired from using your mind on the course and not simply going through the motions, hoping for the best.

Your mind is the tool that will take you from being an ordinary player to becoming a good or great one. When you play golf, you should feel as if you have turned on a switch that frees your mind to focus on the game and block out external issues that you hold within you. Work, school, health, family, and money issues may be flowing through your mind on a daily basis, but to be an accomplished golfer you need to click them off. The moments of breathing and relaxing prior to going to the course will help you free your mind of tension or worry that would interfere with your mental function while you are playing. In the practice section, we will discuss a meditation exercise to use before you leave for the golf course. This meditation will clear your mind and allow it to perform the functions you will need on the course, such as: making strategic decisions; visualizing possibilities; assessing the effects of the elements such as wind, lie, wetness, and cold; creating shots or means of pulling off a particular shot; and thinking how to win against the course or an opponent.

A good golfer's mind is not locked in a grind or drudgery. If that were the case, golf would not be enjoyable and little progress would take place. Your mind should be filled with positive thoughts, your visions set on great shots and scores, a sense of joy and happiness that comes from being accomplished at something that you enjoy. What greater feeling is there than looking at a difficult 20-foot putt, feeling positive that you will make it, and then stepping up to the ball and rolling it into the middle of the cup for a birdie. It is more than just playing a game—it is presenting yourself with a challenge, calling upon your inner being to draw up confidence and self-trust, and then allowing your mind to release and gently direct your muscles to execute exactly what you had envisioned. Golf places you against or with yourself every time you take a club in your hand. You are not playing against someone or something; you are displaying your ability to use the vast assets of your mind to control yourself. Golf is a game of the self because it reflects your inner self.

Golf is not a moral issue, as being a good golfer does not make you a good person, nor does being a bad golfer mark you as a bad person. Being accomplished at winning over yourself, conquering fear, having self-worth and self-esteem as you develop does mark you as having that element of attitude, perseverance, and mental acuity to be able to excel at one of the most difficult games ever created by man. To enjoy life we have needs that must be met as we move through life.

Building a Knowledge Base

To become a good golfer, you must have a good knowledge base about the swing, how to make certain shots, how to strategize against the course or an opponent, how to use and apply the rules of golf, and how to correct mistakes or find help when needed (see p. 19). Many poor players simply do not know how to execute some shots and are doomed to repeat the same faults over and over. If you have ever played with someone who can never hit a shot out of a bunker or when the ball comes out it sails well over the green, you are watching someone who has never learned and practiced how to play a sand shot. The sand shot, for example, is a very easy shot for golfers who know what to do and how to execute the shot. It is so easy that professionals often hope that their wayward shots end up in a bunker rather than in the rough.

Stop and think if there are areas in your game that you simply do not have a clue about to play well. Remember, you are not doomed to be a hacker. Your not knowing how to hit a sand shot now does not mean that you cannot become a master in the sand with some knowledge and practice. Good golfers practice many types of shots, not only to sharpen their skills but to also gain confidence. When the shot or situation arises on the course, they have been there and done that. It is just a case of executing the shot on the basis of the knowledge stored and the physical skills honed in practice. I am not saying that the goal is perfection, as that is impossible for anyone who has ever played the game of golf. The goal is to raise the level of knowledge and proficiency in a significant manner.

Building a good knowledge base comes from a variety of sources that you should seek out to begin your improvement program. Know what to do first and then learn how to do it.

Golf Instruction Books

Some of my favorites include *Five Lessons,* by Ben Hogan; *Golf My Way,* by Jack Nicklaus; and *How I Play the Game,* by Tiger Woods. These and other instruction books are not one-time reads, but should serve as your reference library. When I am having trouble with one portion of my game such as putting, I go back to my books and read the pertinent sections to remind myself of things that I have forgotten or learn drills and techniques that I can use to improve.

One book that is a must read for you is *The Rules of Golf* available from the USGA (usga.com). You must know the rules thoroughly to play at the better levels of golf. The rules are not just restrictions but also offer the golfer options and elements that bring fairness into the game for both you and your opponents. You need to know the rules in order to protect the field or recognize an infraction so other players will not be put at a disadvantage because a partner playing with you violated a rule. You must be able to call a penalty on yourself in golf. Golf may be unique in that it is the only sport in the world in which it is admirable and is common practice to call a penalty and unique to call it on oneself. Your knowledge of the rules can help you get out of a bad situation with little or no penalty, and select options that will make your next shot easier.

Lessons from a Professional

Taking lessons from a golf professional expedites the learning process. Self-learning is important, but it is almost essential that you have someone to guide you along the path to improvement. It's not just that golf professionals are good golfers—we all had to go through training on how to teach golf, correct faults, and offer ways for the student to improve between lessons. So we are also trained as teachers. For some reason men are rather more reluctant that women to take lessons. This may be related to the "asking for directions" gene, but men sometimes see it as a sign of weakness to seek a lesson or ask for help in golf. The very best players in the world, from Tiger Woods on down, all work with teachers on a continual basis.

Find a professional who matches your learning style and with whom you feel comfortable. You can always ask a pro what his or her philosophy of teaching is. Some like to watch and correct; others will build from the ground up; others use visual methods; and yet others teach "by feel"—using their intuition. Ask yourself how you learn best and find a good match for your particular way of learning. Many times women prefer women and men prefer men but there is no restriction on whom you select as your teacher. I take lessons from a wonderful woman teacher, the U.S. Women's Open champion Sandra Palmer. Her methods fit my learning style and I see results from working with her.

In a later chapter we will discuss how to take a lesson and how to benefit from one.

Golf Schools

One of the fastest-growing segments in the area of golf instruction is golf schools. The schools' sessions can run from one to seven days. Group size varies, so you will want to check the school's student-teacher ratio. Also, try to find recommendations or reviews on the school before you sign up for a course. The training is intense and the costs can be high. It is always a good idea to speak with someone who has attended a school and who can tell you how the course was conducted, covering everything from the type and quality of instruction to the accommodations.

I have attended topnotch golf schools in which you come away with a feeling of accomplishment and confidence in the improvement you have made in a short time. I have also attended schools that were very poor and did not meet my needs. Check first to see whether a school is geared to teach at your level, as this is essential.

I have seen players make good progress in a short time at a school. The practice and amount of work and study can be rigorous, so be sure to get yourself in shape to hit a lot of balls and play a lot of golf in a short period. Make sure that your hands are toughened and ready for intense practice. If you do not practice a great deal at home, it may be a good idea to bring a pair of golf gloves so you protect your hands from blisters.

You can research golf schools on the Internet and sometimes find reviews from players who have attended them. Some golf magazines run articles that rate schools. You might find these magazines in your local library.

Magazines

Golf magazines offer great instruction and current updates on equipment and trends that are fun to read and help in building your overall knowledge of the game. My favorites include *Golf Digest*, *Golf Magazine*, *Golf Tips*, and *Golf Illustrated*. These periodicals are a great resource for learning different ways to improve and often offer articles by the very best teachers and touring professionals as they share their thoughts and experience with the reader.

The Internet

There are hundreds and maybe thousands of web sites that offer golf instruction. Do a search on golf instruction, tips, and lessons and you will get a host of places to visit from which you can gain knowledge. Many sites offer videos of great golf swings that you can watch over and over, from the likes of Bobby Jones and Tiger Woods. You can sign up for weekly e-mail newsletters. Some sites offer interactive instruction and advice on a fee basis.

Videos and DVDs

For visual learners videotapes and DVDs are a great way to learn. Those of us raised in the television age have developed visual learning skills, so videos and DVDs are a great resource. These mediums offer you the ability to replay portions over and over again so that you can reinforce your learning. Barnes and Noble (www.bn.com) and Amazon.com stock products of interest to you. Some videos and DVDs focus on particular elements of the game such as putting, the short game, driving, and iron play. Try to find a teacher or touring pro who matches your body build and swing style so that you increase the learning connection. One of my favorite things to do is watch a great swing like Davis Love's or Tom Purtzer's before I go out to play or practice, as the swing rhythm tends to sink in and stay with me much as a song stays in your mind after you have listened to it on your way to work.

Televised Tournaments

Watching touring professionals play under tournament conditions is a great way to gain golf knowledge. While they play at a level few of us will ever know, the way they approach the game—from their pre-shot routines and strategy on a hole to how they swing—are wonderful ways to learn the game. Most stations have excellent professional analysts who offer insights as to how the players attack a hole, what they might be thinking, and even what went wrong when they miss a shot. This is not only entertaining but instructive. Attending a pro tournament in person is a wonderful experience but not as instructional as watching it on television. If you go to a pro tournament, spend a good amount of time near the practice area. This is my favorite thing to do at a tournament. You get to watch the beautiful rhythm of the best golf swings in the world and also get to see practice routines and techniques that may help your own game.

Cable TV Golf Channels

The Golf Channel offers hours of instruction each day from top teachers and is on 24/7. You can set your DVD or VCR to tape instructional shows and build your own library. Most areas also have regional golf telecasts that feature local professionals and courses on a regular basis.

Playing with Good Players

Playing with good players is a must for golfers who want to improve their game. Although you should not hound them with questions, you can learn a great deal by watching how they play. Note their pre-shot routines, the pace of their swings, the strategy they use, and the kinds of shots they play. Notice how they play the holes on your home course to learn the best way to play those holes yourself. Do not be afraid to ask to play with them from time to time. Most good golfers welcome a variety of playing partners and the handicap system will even out the differential. Sign up for tournaments that combine A,B, C, and D players in order to get to play with different players who have good golf skills. Team playing in tournaments will help you learn strategy from the advice given by the A players.

Building a strong knowledge base will help you understand how and why you are doing things in the game. You will have the knowledge of the golf swing and the background to think your way around on a golf course, make correct decisions, and evaluate your options in a myriad of situations that arise in the game. More than other sports, golf offers uniqueness: every golf course is different, every shot is different in some way, no two putts are identical, no two swings are the same, and in almost every round a new situation arises that has never been faced before. Other sports seem predicated on the sameness of action and situation. When something different arises—a triple in baseball or a long run in football—they are reasons to become excited and startled. Golfers on the other hand expect the unexpected and must have a range of knowledge and skills at their disposal in order to succeed.

For you to become a great or even good golfer, possessing a sound knowledge base is not enough in itself. A mathematician or historian can succeed through mastery of a body of theoretical knowledge, but in golf knowing and doing are two separate entities. Affective learning in golf must encompass a desire to improve and become proficient at the game. You must truly want to excel so that as you play you are continually searching and striving to become better. It is a never-ending journey. I feel that the strong desire to excel is what separates golfers who have the same handicap over a period of ten years from the few who make significant changes and steadily get better.

As you start to devote yourself to a program of major improvement in your golf game, you might occasionally wonder: Why make the effort? My thoughts on playing golf to one's highest potential have to do with several factors. First, why spend hours and hours at something that is not enjoyable, like the golfer whom I mentioned above? Golf takes time to play, and hitting good shots, making good scores, and sinking long putts are the rewards of learning and practice. Golf tells you a great deal about yourself every time you set foot on a golf course. How well did you train yourself? How disciplined are you? How do you handle adversity? How do you feel about yourself? How do you deal with friends and competitors? How honest are you? How do you deal with pressure? I recently read an article whose author felt that playing a round of golf should be part of the hiring process for CEOs to get a look at a potential hire in depth and in action. I thought that was a brilliant proposal.

As you play more, your emotional responses may lead to self-discovery. You may find that you have trouble with controlling your anger or frustration or that a two-foot putt under pressure causes you a great deal of anxiety. These are learning opportunities for you in golf and life. In later chapters we will discuss how to recognize and use our emotional and attitudinal framework to help us play better golf. As you begin to learn to become better, be aware of the affective influences that will enter your mind. Acquiring heightened awareness of the stimuli around you and the outside agencies affecting you as well as of your emotions is all part of the total package of being a good player.

Recreation is a vital part of a healthy life. If your recreation time is not pleasant, it is not recreation, so if golf is a task, you should find another avocation. What I hope to instill is a love of the game, not only as a result of being able to play well but also from experiencing the total fascination of the game of golf. The beauty of a golf course is a delight to our senses. Every hole and every course is different. How the architect used the land to blend it with the layout and with nature is a game within the game. I have learned to recognize and learn about species of birds from my fellow golfers and have gone on to read birding books to help enhance the golfing experience. The smell of fresh-cut grass still makes me smile and brings me back to my caddy days as a young boy. Watching a white ball soar against a blue sky is a thrill that has to be felt to be fully appreciated.

Golf is a sport that is steeped in tradition and history. As you go deeper into the game, the names and accomplishments of Jones, Ouimet, Snead, Hogan, Palmer, and Nicklaus take on new dimensions.

The drama and legends surrounding the major tournaments are as enjoyable to read about and watch as the present-day events. The characters, folklore, literature, and art of golf are unparalleled by any other sport. There is spirituality about the game that you will come to know and love. It is a game about life and it is for a lifetime.

In chapter 2 we will go through the basics of the game to include the setup and the swing. We will explore how the mind and body must interact in the psychomotor stage to learn a skill. The goal will be to develop skills based on knowledge but produced through feel and sensory awareness. We cannot rely on knowledge alone to hit a power fade or flop a shot over a bunker and make it stop on a dime. We have to see the shot in our minds, feel it in our hands, and let our muscles and nerves pull the shot off. As we study the "how to" of the game, commit yourself to experiencing the mind-body connection on every shot you learn and hit on the course and in practice. From this day on, you will never hit a shot without an awareness of where it is going and what it should do. This is not a promise that every shot will be a good one; no one who has ever played the game has even approached that goal. You will, however, know what you are doing and will know how to play the game at a level that will give you great satisfaction and enjoyment.

CHAPTER TWO

Steps to Success

IN THIS CHAPTER WE WILL TAKE A STEP-BY-STEP LOOK AT THE ESSENTIALS OF learning the game of golf, from how to hold the club to how to roll a putt. In each section of the putting the game, we will focus on what you need to know, what it looks like, and how it feels. Later on we will discuss how to practice and hone your skills. Remember, no one masters golf, but to become good at the game you must master some fundamentals (grip, stance, posture, and alignment) and have a solid working knowledge of what goes into to the skills so you can acquire them.

The Grip

I have carefully studied the swings of all the top PGA and LPGA players. I have watched videos, seen them in person, and actually have played with some in professional tournaments. Although every swing is different, I noted two things that were similar in only the very best players: the position at impact and the grip.

While some great players had grips that were a little stronger or a little weaker, most had the very same placement of hands on the club. If the grip were not important to a good golf swing, you would see a number of different-looking grips among the best players in the world.

The grip is indeed of significance because it has so much impact on what happens to the club as you swing it. The grip influences how well we can swing a golf club in three major respects:

1. The hands are the only part of the body that touches the club. It is the closest thing we have to controlling the ball. In almost all

other sports, we can put our hands on the ball to control it. In golf, we transmit our control through our hands onto the golf club and then to the ball. Our shoulder turn, hip turn, weight shift—everything we do during the swing to create power and control in the swing—is transmitted to the club head through the grip.

2. The grip directly controls how the face of the club squares to the ball, and this controls accuracy. Scientists tell us that on a drive of 250 yards, if the club face is opened just five degrees it will throw the shot 50 yards off. While this may cause you to worry at first, take comfort in knowing that if you have a proper grip, the club naturally will tend to return to square at impact.

3. The grip allows or restricts the free movement of the rest of your body. Rather like the "tail wagging the dog," your hands can affect the rest of your swing positively or negatively.

Of all the things that can improve your game, the grip will work quickest. When I went through training to become a professional, the first thing we were taught was to focus on the student's grip. If the grip was poor, nothing much was going to happen in the way of improving the golfer's game. The fact that the grip is primarily responsible for getting the club to square at impact is self-explanatory as to how important it is to get it right. At driving ranges or on first tees, I can just look at a player's grip and can tell you what kind of golfer he or she is and what kind of ball flight will ensue. It is not secret psychic power that enables teaching professionals to know this; it is their knowledge of grip positions and their results. In very rare cases will an odd grip produce good results. In these cases, the player makes some kind of adjustment to compensate for the odd grip. Paul Azinger and John Daly, for example, have extremely strong grips but make swing adjustments to get the club square at impact. It is much easier to grip the club conventionally and work from a sound fundamental position than to find ways to compensate.

One of the most intriguing comments about golf, one that has had a lasting impression on me, was made by Jack Nicklaus. Nicklaus observed that about 90 percent of what goes into a golf shot happens before you make the swing. Good pre-shot fundamentals—grip, stance, posture, setup, and mental preparedness, or the "statics," as Nicklaus called them—are all determined at a point we can have the time and ability to exercise complete control over them. During the swing it is difficult to make corrections, but before it, it is within everyone's reach to be as close to perfect as possible. If we get these pre-shot fundamentals in order, we stack the deck in our favor to hit a good golf shot.

We may never have the swings of the top touring professionals but we certainly can copy their fundamentals.

A good grip starts with the amount of pressure we place on the club with our hands. On a scale of 1 to 10 where 1 is hardly holding the club and 10 is a white-knuckled squeeze, a 4 is about right for most players. I try to grip the club so that my forearm muscles are not tensed. This is how I can feel that my grip pressure is about the same each time. A tight grip can restrict the swing dramatically. Most high-handicappers grip the club much too tightly in a false belief that a strong grip on the club will produce distance. In actuality, the lighter your grip, the faster the club head will travel. The primary generator of club-head speed in the golf swing is centrifugal force, not muscle power. A soft grip allows that force to whip the club through impact. To get a sense of how this feels, take a dowel, yardstick, or rod. Grip the stick as tightly as possible in your right hand and swing it along a plane like a golf swing. Now grip the stick with a very light touch and swing it again. You will clearly notice that the soft grip produces a prominent swish noise at the bottom, indicating a much greater speed. The same principle holds true for the golf grip. Always remember this adage: Soft muscles are fast and tight muscles are slow.

A tight grip causes tension as well and tires the muscles out. In baseball, pitchers look at the hands of a hitter. If the hitter's hands are squeezing the bat, the pitcher will take a few extra moments to let the batter's hands grow tired before he delivers a fast ball. In golf, you should combine a soft grip with a little movement of the fingers to grip and re-grip as you are over the ball. This little move, called, "milking the grip" by the pros, relieves tension. The basic idea of a soft grip is that you can feel the club head as you swing and as the club head hits the ball; thus your hands make the important connection.

The grip is so important that by moving the fingers just slightly or adding pressure on certain fingers, you can cause the ball to fly right or left. Good players will modify their grip during a round to work the ball or to make sure the club stays square in certain lies: they will tighten the last three fingers on the left hand to produce a fade to the right, or turn both hands to the left on the grip in the sand so the club face does not close in the sand. It stands to reason to get your hands in the right position from the start.

Let's take a look at the three types of grips in golf.

The Overlapping Grip

The overlapping grip is the one used by the vast majority of top touring professionals and leading amateur golfers. Do not assume, however, that this is automatically the best grip for you. This grip is characterized by the little finger of the right hand nestling into the crevice created between the first and second fingers of the left hand. This grip offers a feeling of oneness in the hands, as they feel molded together. There is also good flexibility in the wrists as this grip does not tense the forearm muscles. This grip is best for players who have strong hands and good control of the fingers. I prefer this grip as it feels very comfortable to me and seems easy to learn and stay with throughout your golfing career. (It is sometimes called the Vardon grip because it was introduced by the golf professional Harry Vardon at the turn of the twentieth century.)

The Interlocking Grip

The interlocking grip is the next most popular grip in golf. This grip was one of the original ways to grip the club in the game's early history before Vardon introduced the overlapping grip. Many players today use the interlocking grip—Jack Nicklaus and Tiger Woods are two who have done pretty well with it. Many LPGA professionals use the interlocking as it favors people who have smaller hands.

In this grip the little finger of the right hand is actually locked between the first two fingers of the left. Players who favor this grip like the feeling of having the right hand securely in place on the grip throughout the swing. The right hand will not let go at the top of the swing or at follow-through. It makes sense that Tiger Woods uses this grip as it is the only one that can keep his hands on the club at his swing speed. The key is that this grip helps all players keep their hands in place and helps the hands work together very well.

The Ten-Finger Grip

In the ten-finger grip, all ten fingers are on the club much as a baseball player holds a bat. This grip has made a great comeback recently within the Natural Golf movement, which emphasizes that this grip is the natural way to place your hands on a golf club. Moe Norman (PGA Tour, 1959–60), the great Canadian player, used the ten-finger grip to win many professional tournaments, and many historians claim that Norman was the greatest ball striker of all time. If you choose to follow the Natural Golf method, this grip flows in the sequence of things used in that concept. Youngsters should start with the ten-finger grip, as their hands are not big or strong enough to handle the overlapping or interlocking grips. For adults, however, I would suggest the overlapping or interlocking grips as the ten-finger grip may make your hands work against each other—which is good in baseball but not in golf.

Gripping the Club

While watching the PGA Tour recently, I have noticed more and more players checking their grips in their pre-shot routine. Some players even go through a little grip-check drill such as is often used with beginning students in a golf lesson. This shows me that the very best players are paying more and more attention to the details of the fundamentals instead of just feeling what is comfortable and winging it on the course. It is important that you, too, grip the club the same way every time you set up to the ball. You can have a perfect grip for every shot if you take a few seconds to make sure that your hands are placed correctly on the club. When things start going haywire on the course, it may simply be that you have become a little sloppy on how you are holding the club. Sometimes we can become distracted by wind, our lie, or the pin placement and forget to make the little check on our grip. Make a promise to yourself to build in a little grip check before you make a swing both in practice and on the course. I have watched pilots go through a meticulous preflight check of every detail in the cockpit just to be perfectly sure that everything is shipshape for the flight. Of course the consequences are far more important in flying than on a golf course, but it does serve as a good example of getting things right before you start up your engine. Once you practice the pre-shot grip check it will become a habit that requires no conscious effort but will pay immediate dividends in your playing well.

A comfortable grip is certainly a factor, but the most important aspect of the grip is control. You want to grip the club so that the club head goes where it is supposed to go naturally. An awkward grip may cause you to make some kind of odd adjustment in your swing. Gripping the club in a neutral or slightly strong manner is the best way to set your hands. Once you learn a good fundamental grip, you can make refinements with the help of a professional. Let's run through the steps of taking hold of a club that is common among the top players:

1. Stand up straight with both hands at your sides and let the club fall naturally into your left hand. The club should be held in the fingers and along the line where they meet the hand.

2. Lay the sole, or bottom of the club head, on the ground in front of you so that it lies flat. The club face should be square to your target. Often, amateurs make the mistake of trying to align the club face while it is in the air. It is almost impossible to aim at a target this way.

3. Let the grip of the club run across your left hand from the knuckle of your first finger to the fleshy part of your hand. The fleshy part of your left hand is actually a strong muscle that offers

strength and control for you in swinging the club. The three fingers of your left hand should secure the club against the inside of your hand and not hold the club by themselves.

4. Roll your left hand over on top of the shaft and place your thumb so that it is in the "one o'clock" position if you look down at it. Do not make the common mistake of running the thumb straight down the shaft as this will cause restriction and not allow the wrists to hinge up and down during the swing. Extend the thumb down so that it lies naturally on the grip. Avoid stretching it down or notching it up.

5. Place your right hand on the club by interlocking or overlapping your little finger first, then roll your hand over gently to the top of the shaft. Do not make any twisting or grabbing motions in order to keep the club face square.

6. Place your right thumb in the "11 o'clock" position as you look down. Let the thumb rest gently on the side of the shaft with no pressure.

Now let's go through the steps to check your grip:

1. On both hands, the gap between your thumb and forefinger should form a V. The V's of both hands should point to the right side of your face.

2. Look at the positions of your thumbs so that they have remained in the clock positions mentioned above.

3. The palms of your hands should face each other.

4. The grip should be light enough so there is no tension in your hands or forearms.

Good Hands

Good golfers have hands that are strong yet very supple. You can strengthen your hands by squeezing a rubber ball or hand spring. This will build the muscles in your hands and forearms to help you maintain control and deliver power. To increase suppleness, I like to stretch my hands before practicing or playing. I place my hands on a table with my fingers extended and the palms down. I gently slide the palms down and spread the fingers so that I feel a stretch in all the fingers and muscles of the hands. Relax your arms at your sides and shake your hands out. You should feel a relaxed and tension-free sensation in both hands. This not only helps you soften your feel before playing but also serves as a mental cue to grip the club lightly and correctly for the rest of the day.

Most players wear a golf glove (on the left hand if they're right-handed, and vice versa) when they play. A golf glove will offer better traction on the grip and help resist slipping or twisting during the swing. On hot, steamy days change your glove so that you are always playing with a dry one. Take the glove off between shots to let your hands air. As you play, avoid carrying a club and constantly swinging or fidgeting with it. This habit tends to tire out your hands over the course of the round. Let your hands relax and feel soft.

As you begin your program of improvement, keep learning the feel of a good grip. Look at pictures of the grips of great players and imitate the way the hands lie on the club. Check yourself in a mirror to see what your grip looks like: the V's should point toward the right side of your face. As you watch television, have a club handy and grip and re-grip the club over and over to learn the feel so that a good grip becomes natural and you won't have to figure it out each time on the course.

Set Yourself Up for Great Golf

Recently I watched a touring pro being interviewed after a round. The interviewer asked, "How important are fundamentals?" The touring pro looked a little puzzled as the answer seemed obvious to him—but maybe not to many players across the country. The touring pro simply said, "Without good fundamentals, too many things can go wrong."

That statement speaks volumes about the importance of the setup in golf. If you set up to the ball with everything in place, your chances of hitting a good shot increase dramatically. The slices, wild hooks, and topped and fat shots can often be traced back to your setup to the ball and not to the actual swing itself. Once you accept this thought, you are well on your way to becoming a better player. Master the fundamentals and the door opens for major improvement. Your devotion to learning the fundamentals is a measure of your commitment to becoming a good golfer. You must work on the fundamentals in practice and on the course on every shot. Later, when we discuss practice, we will establish a routine for you to follow.

If you watch the average golfer on the course, you will often see the same pre-shot routine. She will check the yardage to the green, take a practice swing, step up to the ball, take one look at the green, and then fire away. The same player on the practice tee will hit a shot, rake another ball over, and fire away in machine-gun style until all the balls are gone. In both instances, there is no real concentration or mental awareness of what has to be done and how to do it. This, I feel, is one of the main reasons why golfers seldom improve during their golfing lives.

To set up for success, set up to the ball with a clear idea of what factors are influencing the shot, how you are going to make the swing, and, most important, what it will look like before you swing. The pre-shot routine is the time to run through and set the conditions for success. The elements that must be taken into consideration are as follows;

- Shot strategy
- Course/lie considerations
- Club selection
- Aim
- Alignment
- Ball position
- Stance

Do not be concerned that with this pre-shot routine you will hold up the course for hours. You can run through these steps in your mind and then step up to the ball and be ready to go when it's your turn to play. These steps are primarily mental actions that make you concentrate and calculate accurately and then place your body in the position to execute the shot. Remember what Nicklaus said as you work on the pre-shot routine: "Ninety percent of a good golf shot happens before the swing."

Shot Strategy

Shot strategy is the how and where of the golf shot. Every shot should be planned and not left up to the golf gods. The good golfer expects a good shot and knows what it should look like. The average golfer is hoping for a good shot but certainly does not truly expect one. He is focused mainly on direction, whereas the good golfer is thinking in terms of scoring. The very best players rehearse the shot in advance by mentally feeling their swing and visualizing the shot that must be played. It may be a high shot that lands softly or a low running one that bounces and rolls onto the green. Whatever it takes to score well is the guiding principle in what kind of shot to hit.

Visualization is a mental technique that can take your game to a higher level. By visualizing your swing and "seeing" the ball fly and land as you want it to you can program your mind and body to perform the correct action. If you watch gymnasts, skaters, and divers just before they launch into action, you will see them in a state of deep concentration that is almost trancelike. What they are doing is actually viewing themselves performing their action to perfection while their body senses what it has to do. Called psychomotor planning, this process builds a true mind-body connection by synchronizing the mind and body. Great players in all sports visualize before executing. Jack Nicklaus characterized visualization as "going to the movies."

The power of visualization cannot be underestimated. In one famous sports psychology study, scientists took a group of high school basketball players and broke them into three groups to test the development of free-throw skills. One group practiced making free throws for one hour per day for thirty days. The second group did not practice making any free throws. The third group also did not actually practice free throws but simply visualized making them for one hour per day. After the month was over, the scientists were quite surprised at the results: The group that practiced every day increased its success rate by about 10 percent. The group that did not practice at all saw its skills fall off about 10 percent. The surprise? The group that just visualized making the free throws actually improved 10 percent, like the players who practiced every day!

You do not have to have special powers to become good at visualization. It is a mental skill that you can and should learn. In graduate school we were taught how to visualize by beginning with the known and moving to the unknown. Start by finding a quiet place and closing your eyes. Quiet your mind and relax any noise in your head. Now try to visualize you're the front door of your house. Get a big picture first and look at it. Notice the colors, any chipped paint, decoration or things that make your door stand out. Look at the door knob and note the color and see if you can feel it in your mind. Open your door and see what is behind it as you have seen it hundreds or thousands of times before.

If you can do this exercise you can master the skill of visualization. Practice visualizing things in your life such as driving to work, talking with your boss, and performing your everyday tasks. You will notice a few things; for one thing, you will start to notice details in your life that you never saw clearly before, from objects to interactions between people. This means your awareness is being heightened. Another result of visualization is that your performance or interaction will improve because you have already rehearsed it in your mind, much as an actor rehearses before a play.

Before playing in a round that I feel that I must execute well, I rely heavily on meditation and visualization long before I get to the course. In a recent tournament I was in the last pairing of the day. I woke up and went to a beach alone at about 5 A.M. I sat on the beach and watched the sun rise over the water while I relaxed my mind and envisioned a smooth golf swing and set myself in a calm, confident mood. When I got to the course to warm up I was completely relaxed and free of any nervousness or anxiety. I only had to trust my swing and see the shots that I needed to hit. I shot a 74 in tough conditions to finish up among the leaders. The round was the product of setting my mind up to play well and not simply relying on my muscles to hit good shots.

Scientists have stated that we are only beginning to scratch the surface of the power of our minds. Using your mind to learn in a holistic, multisensory way is an untapped tool for most of us. Changing your approach to use your mind to play better golf and control your thinking will give you a new perspective on achieving your goals in golf and life. The world's great athletes may not be geniuses, but they do think and focus at another level than most of the rest of the population. The Russians in the 1970s realized this and created a sports institute for their athletes that combined physical and mental training to bring them to peak performance.

There is in all of us a direct link between mind and body. When we make a change in our minds it transfers a change to the body; converesely, a change in our physiology will be reflected by an attitudinal change. Through practice that integrates the mind and body the attitudinal change that usually occurs is confidence and trust. The very best players have confidence flowing around them like an aura. Watch Tiger Woods when he is near the lead in a tournament. He seems so sure of himself that it must intimidate anyone playing with him. It is not brash cockiness or braggadocio; it is a quiet, unseen, unheard phenomenon that lies within and comes out as presence.

Enhancing your mental abilities to gain that trust and confidence in yourself begins with visualization. You can use visualization in two distinct ways on the course to develop strategy. The first use helps you plan your shots. Look at the hole ahead of you and visualize the best way to play it. Think in terms of the easiest way to make par and not some risky, go-for-broke birdie attempt. See your drive land in a spot that will give you the best approach angle to the hole. Next see the shot to the green and the part of the green where you will need to land and how the ball should travel to that area. Then visualize the putt that you have for your birdie and if you miss where to leave it for a tap-in par.

You will also use visualization to produce a good swing—from behind your ball as you see yourself hit the ball and watch it fly to the exact spot that you have selected. In this visualization you will actually want to feel the swing as you envision yourself hitting the shot. Feel the impact of club and ball and watch the ball fly into the sky and land in your chosen spot. When you step up to the ball for real, you already know and expect what is going to happen. There are no thoughts of water, rough, out of bounds, or any negative thoughts whatsoever in your mind. You have a quiet confidence and can trust your swing to perform because your mind is quiet and knows how to communicate to your body.

One of the best golfers that I have ever played with would walk up to his putts with a tiny grin on his face. He never mentioned what he was thinking about and I never asked, so as not to interfere with something that may have been subconscious and private in his own pre-shot routine. I am sure, however, that he had such a level of inner confidence that in his mind he could see the putt drop into the hole and that thought brought him a feeling of elation before the actual event had taken place. Visualization is seeing the shot the way you want to play it. It is the complete opposite of wishing and hoping for a good shot. You are setting yourself up to hit a shot with predetermined focus and accuracy. Just by doing this, you will not only increase your percentage for success but you will reduce the chance of failure to a minimum.

Pre-shot Considerations

Before playing a shot, you must analyze the elements that the course and the particular shot present to you. First of all, you are going to get good and bad breaks on the course. The good and bad never seem to even out, but I think this is a misperception. We tend to remember the bad breaks and talk about them and dismiss the good ones as they fall under our false assumption that we will always hit a good shot. The important thing to remember is to play what is given to you and in practice prepare for all contingencies. If your 300-yard drive lands in a divot, it should not be seen as a jinx but rather as a challenge to demonstrate your skill and composure. In other words, always deal from strength rather than weakness.

Course and Lie Conditions

Understanding the effects of course and lie conditions is a matter of experience and judgment. Wind, wetness, texture of the greens, slope of the land areas of trouble—consider how all of these will have an impact on your shot. An approach shot to a hard, dry green is substantially different from one to a wet, soft one. How you play the shot is dictated by the conditions that you face. The most important factor to consider immediately is how your ball is sitting on the ground, for this affects how your club head will be able to strike the ball and what the ball will do once it is airborne. A ball becomes airborne when it becomes trapped on the grooves of your club face and spins backward—this causes it to lift into the air. Spin lifts it high. The direction of the ball's flight is determined by the angle at which the club face strikes the ball and the position on the club face where contact is made. If grass comes between your club face and ball, the ball will not spin as much and may fly through the air farther than you expected. A side-hill lie might cause the club face to angle in or out at impact and send the ball off in the wrong direction. Later on we will discuss how to handle particular lies and conditions, but for now, take the lie and conditions into consideration as you approach your ball.

Club Selection

Selecting the right club for your shot is critical to getting the ball to your target. Too many golfers seem to rely on yardage alone as the main criterion in selecting a club. If they are standing next to the 150-yard marker, some players automatically reach for a seven-iron as they feel that it is their 150-yard club. For one thing, the 150-yard marker, if accurate, is only a measure of distance to the middle of the green. Some greens may have a three-club difference. While a solid seven-iron might get you to the middle of the green, a pin in the back will require a six-iron, whereas a pin up-front might call for an eight-iron. Other considerations include such things as wind strength and direction. The wind can cause your ball to come up way short or fly well over the green. Factor in the effect of wind when you choose your clubs. For example, a strong wind might be called a two-club wind. This means that if the wind is against you, you need to hit a club that is two clubs longer than normal, and vice versa if the wind is behind you.

Elevation also plays a significant role in club selection. We look at the pin as the crow flies, but the crow may be flying down or up to the green. A good rule of thumb is to select one more club for every 10 yards of elevation and subtract a club when heading downhill. If you are hitting to an elevated green, forget the yardage marker, because you must land the ball on the green—it will not bounce and roll to a pin that is above you.

Look at the terrain near your target area. Firing directly at the pin may not be the best option for many shots. If the green has a severe slope, see how you can either use or avoid the slope to get the best results once your ball lands and begins to roll. If the pin is protected by a bunker or water, play to a safe spot and do not gamble on making a high number by taking a risky shot. If the front of the green slopes back toward you—a feature in so many modern courses—avoid the trap of landing on the front and hoping for a bounce back to the pin. This is called a false front and is designed to deceive the golfer. As you grow in experience and learn from reading, watching, and playing, you will add to your knowledge base. Try to learn something every time you play and every time you watch a professional tournament.

Another important consideration is your own size, skill, and swing speed. Golfers all hit their clubs at different distances; hit the club that fits *your* game and will get *your* ball to the target. A 150-yard shot is not a seven-iron for everybody. Men seem to equate how far or what iron they hit for a shot with their manhood. As a result, most of the time they come up short and say they didn't hit the shot cleanly. In truth, they chose the wrong club.

The key is to know how far *you* hit each club. Swallow your pride and play the club that is right for you for the specific target. One time I was hitting balls at Doral Golf Resort in Miami, Florida, next to a PGA touring pro, Hank Kuene. I was hitting my driver very well and was pleased to see the ball land toward the other end of the range. Hank was hitting five-irons beyond what I was getting with my driver. This was a point well taken for me. When I get to my ball and try to determine what club to hit, I do get a yardage, but I do not use that as the basis of club selection. Instead, I use a method that works perfectly for me. You may use it as well. I look at the target along a straight line. First I imagine where a nine-iron would land the ball along the line if I hit it correctly; then I envision an eight-iron; then a seven-; etc., until I can visualize the club that brings the ball right to the target. By using this method, you automatically factor in many elements. First, you are selecting a club on the basis of how far you actually hit the ball and not what someone else would hit or thinks you should hit. The wind or rain and the slope and texture of the green are accounted for in one thought process. You will come to know your distances from practice and experience.

Aim and Alignment

Aiming at your target and aligning your body are not as simple as they sound. Most players think that they are lined up correctly when in fact they are far off. The problem is our eyes. It's not that they are bad; it is because they are so good. Our eyes always find the straight line to the target. Where we err is in placing the club head and then aligning our feet, hips, and shoulders. When we just look at the target, we see a straight line to the pin. We could look back over our shoulder and still see straight to the target. What we need to do is build a connection between our eyes and our aim.

The way about 90 percent of golfers take aim and align is to stand over the ball, sight down the line, and adjust the feet. It simply does not work. The best way to aim and align is to stand behind the ball and mentally draw a big white line back from the target to your ball. This is your target line. My pre-shot routine includes an effective aiming and aligning technique. Select a small object about one foot in front of your ball along the target line and set the club face so that it points directly to that object. You then place your feet, hips, and shoulders parallel to the short target line created by the ball and the small object in front of the ball. This technique will become an essential part of your pre-shot routine.

To align yourself properly, you need to build your sighting skills. In practice, stand behind your ball and mentally draw that white line to your target. Lay a two-by-four just outside of your ball so that it points toward the target. Take a club and lay it down where the tips of your feet will be in your stance. The two shafts should be parallel. Step up to the ball and place your toes so that they are just inside and parallel to the shaft near your feet. Check your hips and shoulders to see if they too are square along the target line and not twisted. It is a good idea to have a friend or a pro stand behind you to check to see that you are aligned and aiming properly. If you do this every time you practice, you mental skills associated with aim and alignment will increase and you will set up much more easily on the course.

When you practice such things as alignment, you benefit in several ways. You will now know how to line yourself up so that it is no longer a worry or source of wonder when you are playing. Another benefit is confidence. You will know that you have done everything in your power to aim directly at your target, and now all that is left is pull the trigger and make the swing. Practicing learning how to aim and align will show results almost immediately. If you have been missing greens on a regular basis, the element of proper alignment could be the reason. Using these techniques you will perfect your aim and alignment and remove these defects from your game.

One additional note on aim and alignment relates to hitting your tee shot. If a genie came out of a bottle and offered to grant me either distance or accuracy on my tee shots, I would choose accuracy without hesitation. Almost anyone can smash a ball a good distance, but you can't score well playing from deep rough and woods all day. I will take a shot in the fairway every time and know that I will score well. In setting up for your tee shot, remember that the world is not your oyster. Many golfers just see a big fairway and smash the ball in the general direction of the short grass—with poor results. On the tee shot, use the same care and pinpoint alignment that you would use when going after a pin. Select a spot in the fairway that will offer you the best shot into the green and set your second shot up for success. On holes that are very narrow or ones that pose a lot of trouble, use a fairway wood or iron and aim at the middle of the fairway as if it were the only thing that you can see off of the tee. On blind tee shots, or ones where you cannot see where the ball will land, select a distant tree or even a cloud as your alignment target. Avoid using the tee markers or the tee itself to align yourself. The tee and tee markers will often point you in the wrong direction. Align yourself as if they do not exist.

Ball Position

My students often ask me about the ball position: where the ball should be placed in the stance. Another question is how far to stand from the ball and where to look while swinging. I wish there were some hard and fast answers to these questions, but there is no one way to do these things in golf. Some great players play all of their shots from one ball position, such as opposite their left heel, and then they adjust the width of the stance depending on the length of the club. I have tried this method but it does not feel comfortable to me and does not seem logical. Since clubs come in different lengths they will bottom out at different places despite how wide or narrow your stance. I was taught by some top professionals to play my shots somewhere between my left armpit (driver) and the middle of my chest (wedge and nine-iron). This ball-positioning system seems to accommodate the length of the shafts and the spot where the clubs would naturally strike the ground. The other clubs should fall in between.

One good way to set your ball position correctly every time is to step up to the ball with your feet together and just opposite the ball. Move your left foot down the target line to get the exact placement of the ball that you want and then move your right foot back naturally for balance. If you do this every time, you will always have correct ball position and you will take the guesswork out of a complicated fundamental.

Your distance from the ball depends on your height and build. In general, you should be able to place a hand or fist between the butt end of the club and your body. I like to feel my arms hanging down from my shoulders with no tension. Doing this ensures that I am not reaching for the ball, nor do I have my hands too close to my body.

The hands do not actually hang down straight but actually tend to fall under your head or chin as you hold the club. Letting your arms fall from your shoulders is for feel. You can set your ball position by taking a five-iron and making natural swings without a ball and see where the club takes a divot. Set your other club positions by noting that the five-iron is in the middle of your ball-position line, and the driver and pitching wedge are at the two outer edges of the line, respectively.

Taking Your Stance

Your guiding as you learn the proper stance for golf is: Everything in moderation. Look at a crowded driving range and I guarantee that you will see the extremes of stances. Some players bend their knees so much they look as though they are sitting on a chair. There are those who reach out for the ball so far that you wonder whether they will hit it with the club. Then there are others who are as straight and stiff as West Point cadets. Perhaps at some point a teaching pro or friend told them to bend their knees at address, or to stand taller, and they figured that if a little bend is good then a lot is better, or taller means straight up.

A good setup position is one that places you to make an athletic move. A good stance will allow you to maintain balance, swing the club back and forth on a good plane, and allow you to strike the ball solidly from power generated from a turn and good foot action. Think of how, in baseball, a shortstop would set himself to be ready: head up, knees bent, weight centered and balanced toward the balls of his feet, back bent from the hips, and staring straight with arms hanging freely. The golf stance and setup is very much like that of the shortstop. You should build the fundamentals of a good setup when you practice and check your stance every time in your pre-shot routine.

The placement of the feet in your stance serves two purposes, alignment and balance. The width between the feet directly affects your ability to make a proper turn during the swing. As you practice setting up correctly, always think in terms of obtaining a free and loose feeling; avoid anything that feels restrictive. Some positive changes will feel different—maybe a little awkward—but never restrictive.

Players often take an overly wide stance as this seems to give them a sense of power. It doesn't work, though. To test this, take an exaggeratedly wide stance, with your feet about three inches outside your shoulders. Now take a swing with your driver. You will quickly find that it is very difficult to turn your shoulders and hips and move your legs in support of the club. You would probably never take a stance this wide while playing, but it is a fact that many golfers do take a stance that restricts their swing. I think that a wide stance comes from our early days of playing baseball. In baseball, the swing arc is horizontal and requires a wider stance to support the path of the bat as it travels during the swing. Power hitters often have wide stances. In golf, however, the swing is more of a vertical plane and requires support that is more centered, toward the middle of the swing, where the club travels at its greatest speed. A commonsense approach to the width of a stance in golf is to place your feet under your shoulders as you set up with your driver. This width places your feet and legs as poles under the massive parts of your body and offers the balance to support the club while allowing you to pivot on both feet during the swing. As clubs decrease in length, your stance should grow narrower.

Your back foot provides a kick or pushing-off motion during the move through impact, and it should be almost perpendicular to your target line. Similarly, a baseball pitcher pushes off of the rubber on the mound as he throws a pitch. The back foot will actually push off to create power and come up on the toe at the finish to provide balance. It is perfectly acceptable to flare the back foot out a little for comfort, but do not overdo it. Golfers who have a Charlie Chaplin stance, with both toes well flared out, tend to fall back on their heels and have poor balance.

The front foot should be flared out slightly, the toe angled a bit toward the target. This little move helps to prevent overswinging on the backswing and also provides a solid platform for the weight shift onto the front foot during the impact-to-follow-through parts of the swing. Again, moderation is the key, and there are nuances to learn. Some talented players turn their front foot inward to promote a ball flight that hooks and open it up to help create a fade. You might practice this later as you develop more golf skills—I mention it here as an example of what foot positioning can mean for your golf shot. The key in taking the stance is to be consistent. Practice the same width for a particular club on each shot. High-handicappers seem to vary their stance from shot to shot and naturally have inconsistent results. Golf is a sport that offers a myriad of situations and shots, but consistency in the setup and swing must be achieved if you are to make significant gains.

The next element of a good setup is to have a slight break in the knees so that your legs feel soft and ready to move during the swing. Both stiff knees and knees that are bent too much are tension builders and swing killers. Just flex your knees to set them in a ready position. Bend from your hips, not your waist, so that your back is straight and you are set slightly forward so that your arms can move freely during the swing. A straight back allows you to swing on a correct plane, prevents dipping up and down, and allows you to make a full, powerful shoulder turn. In several instructional books I have read that you should have the sensation of sitting on a bar stool. This is bad advice as you cannot maintain good balance from a position that has your butt placed so far back. Whoever wrote that tip in the first place was probably sitting on a bar stool at the time.

As we mentioned in the discussion of alignment, your feet, hips, and an imaginary line between the shoulders should all point parallel to the target line. Once you set up to the ball, you should tap your feet up and down and move your legs a little to break tension. In fact, you should never really become perfectly still but should make subtle movements to keep a free-flowing feeling throughout your body and mind—which doesn't mean to get happy feet that move all over the place and throw your alignment out.

Another thing that I often see is something I call "Bob, the golfer." Bob takes his stance and then bobs up and down to look at the target. Each time that he bobs he sets himself in a different head position where he is too far from or close to the ball. Instead of bobbing up and down to check your target when you are over the ball, simply swivel your head and return it to the ball. Watch the touring pros and you will see how they look at the target without moving out of position.

The Pre-shot Routine

Being consistent comes from repeating the same things over and over so that no new element can enter your mind or body. Building a good pre-shot routine will bring consistency to your game. No longer will you have a bad shot followed by a good one and wonder what happened. Later in this book we will discuss how to practice a pre-shot routine and make it the bridge between the practice range and the course. Let's run through the steps of a proven pre-shot routine that can be yours for the rest of your life:

1. Stand behind your ball and breathe deeply by expanding your stomach on the inhale and retracting it on the exhale. Look at the target and sight down the line to where you want to hit the ball. Pick a spot about one foot in front of your ball (a divot, bit of discolored grass, leaf, or twig) that lies on the line between your ball and the target) and keep your eyes on that spot for a moment.

2. Make a smooth practice swing while looking at your target and visualize yourself hitting the ball and watching it fly to your target.

3. Walk slowly up to the ball and set the club face so that it points directly at the interim target, the little spot in front of your ball, as if it were a one-foot putt. Step up to the ball while looking at the target and align your body to the point where your club face is aiming.

4. Take your grip and check it, waggle your club up and down or back and forth with a light feeling to gain a sense of feel. Check the target once more, then set your eyes on the back of the ball and start your backswing in a smooth motion.

The two most important elements in the pre-shot routine are to have a clear idea of what is going to happen with the shot and to be completely relaxed and confident in your ability to hit the shot. You can modify this pre-shot routine to suit your own needs and sense of becoming comfortable and focused. Some top players dangle the club in their right hand freely as they walk to the ball. This helps develop a feeling for the club head and promotes an overall sense of lightness and feel. This is the time to remove all anxiety or negative thought about the shot or yourself. Walk up to the ball with trust and confidence that comes from practice and a developed mind.

I have made two observations while watching touring professionals' pre-shot routines. One is that they look at the target more than they look at the ball. High handicappers become almost ball bound. They stand over the ball for a long time, fixating on it as tension and anxiety creep into their bodies. Does a baseball pitcher look at the ball just before he throws it? Does a basketball player stare at the ball before shooting a free throw? Does a soccer player glare at the ball before kicking a goal? Of course not. These athletes are target-oriented. They have trained their minds to deliver their shots to the target and trust their physiological skills to carry out their mind's directions.

The second observation is that the touring pros have a look of being completely focused on the task ahead. Their whole being is locked in the moment of producing a great shot. They are not looking around, fiddling with their equipment or clothes, or talking as they step up to the ball and settle themselves over it. They evince relaxed, quiet concentration with the emphasis on staying in the moment, not grinding or bitter determination, which taxes the mind. Nothing in the past or future is allowed to have an impact on their emotional state as they get ready to play the shot.

Some golf psychologists have referred to the role of the "inner eye," in golf and in other situations in life. A simple definition of the inner eye is "the ability to see things without your eyes." One example of this is when you look at a lighted room, then close your eyes. You will still be able to "see" where everything is, using your inner eye. In golf, you can use your inner eye to build a link between you and your target. Once you are over the ball for a shot or a putt, look at the target and then back at your ball. Hold the picture of the target in your mind's eye while you make your swing. Some of the benefits of this are that you will gain greater accuracy and greatly enhance your distance control. Later, we will discuss how you can develop your inner eye on the practice tee. Do not try this on the course without practicing it first on the range, as it takes a degree of mind control to get used to doing it during the golf swing.

That warning reminds me of something funny that happened when I was playing with four amateurs in a scramble-type tournament. We had a downhill short pitch to a green that sloped away from us. I went first and hit a high flop shot (a risky shot) that floated into the air, landed softly, and rolled gently down the slope. The captain of the team looked at the other players and said, "Don't any of you guys try that." One player replied, "I know. He is a professional on a closed course."

Building a Swing

Ben Hogan once said, "Golf cannot be taught, only learned." To build a swing that will produce the results that you want, you have to become a total learner. Involve your knowledge base, develop your appreciation for a great swing, and work to develop the feel of a great swing. Make the swing a goal that you set for yourself, and devote everything you do in your golf life toward reaching that goal. Write it down; put it on the refrigerator door!

My Goal: *To develop a consistent, fundamentally sound golf swing that yields good results.*

Writing down the goal helps you keep it in front of you as you play and practice, watch the professionals, and read about the swing. It will help you concentrate and keep what is important to becoming a better player at the forefront. If you visit a driving range and see golfers hit one ball after another in every possible direction, you are watching people who do not really have a goal in mind as they practice. They may be having fun and maybe that is all that they want, which is fine. Getting to be a good golfer is another story. Even watching a professional tournament on television should take on a different perspective for you. Enjoy the drama of the tournament and follow the leaders with anticipation, but also pay careful attention to the swings that are made as well as the strategy employed. Watch every golf swing as if it were a private lesson. Try not to be analytical but drink the swing into your mind so that the rhythm, tempo, posture, and positions are loaded into your mind's library.

Just watching a great golf swing can make you a better player. I once read about a club professional who spent a one-day workshop at the U.S. Golf Association headquarters in Far Hills, New Jersey, watching "Iron Byron," the mechanical swing machine, hit balls most of the day. The next day the pro went out and broke the course record at his home course. He theorized that watching the machine (which was patterned on Byron Nelson's swing) had somehow embedded the swing in his mind. Later on we will show you ways of developing great swing mechanics from visualization and other visual learning techniques.

We can't learn a good golf swing just through reading, watching, or instruction. Yet these are the basic groundwork for learning the swing fundamentals. Without know what a good golf swing entails, you will never have one. Golf swings are like snowflakes in that no two are perfectly alike. However, if you watch the very best players, you will see that their swings are very similar in many ways. To begin building your knowledge base, watch a great golf swing.

Select a professional as your model. Find a player who is similar to you in build and swing tempo. Your model should have a swing that is very sound and one that you can copy using photos and videos. Tiger Woods has a tremendous swing, but he isn't necessarily a good model: Tiger is young, strong, and flexible and possesses incredible timing to coordinate the parts of his body while swinging at 125 miles per hour. Few people could ever copy it with any chance of capturing it for themselves.

Some players who have wonderful golf swings and are of more average physical proportions are David Toms, Tom Purtzer, Annika Sorenstam, Nick Price, Karrie Webb, Tom Watson, and Hale Irwin. These players' swings have a transparency that lets you see how fundamentally sound they are throughout the swing. Some great players make corrections en route to impact and these swings are not suitable as models. Lee Trevino, Arnold Palmer, Jim Furyk, Nancy Lopez, and John Daly are a few that come to mind. You will be watching every aspect of the swing, and a good model is one where you can focus on great positions at all points in the swing.

To learn rhythm and tempo in the golf swing, I suggest that you watch the LPGA professionals. The women do not have the muscles to hit the ball a long way with accuracy. They must rely on perfect contact more than their male counterparts. To do this, the swing must be smooth, designed to deliver the club head perfectly square at impact. Freddie Couples and Ernie Els are known for their tempo, but they both have swing speeds that are well beyond the normal player's realm, a result of the torque that they develop in their shoulder turns.

Once you select your model player (see http://www.beauproductions.com/golfswingsws/), gather videos, DVDs, stop-action photo sequences, and any articles on your chosen one. You can tape a tournament and then edit it so that you can watch only your model play his or her shots. An advantage of videos and DVDs is that you can watch the swing in slow motion and also stop the swing at different positions. Another way to watch the swing is to advance the video one frame at a time. This was my preferred way of copying a swing. This way of developing a swing is a great starting point and one that helps you absorb the swing without thinking of where your left hip is at a certain point. Your aim is to gain a holistic picture of a wonderful golf swing and plant it in your mind. As you practice, think and feel that pro's swing as if it had been transferred into your body. This is a proven way to develop and learn. Children can do this with ease because they are in a learning mode. You need to make up your mind to place yourself in the same mode and get out of your way when learning.

Many years ago I copied Gene Littler's swing to develop my game. People who watch my swing often compliment me on the apparent ease in my rhythm and tempo, and I think back to the hours I put in watching videos and stop-action photos of Littler before I went to practice. I even brought the photos with me to the practice range and posed in front of a mirror while looking back at the photos as I imitated positions. I once chatted with Gene Littler and told him what I had done. He smiled at the amount of effort I had put into copying his swing and was happy to hear that I had done well with it.

Learning the Swing in Steps

There are different ways of learning. I have chosen to present learning the golf swing in a way that was easy for me to learn; it is based on proven studies of learning approaches.

First we choose a model and absorb the whole of the swing. This is a wonderful starting point as it puts the goal visually in front of you. In other words, you know what David Toms's swing looks like and that is your visual goal. Let your mind keep the whole concept of the model swing throughout your learning. Then we break the swing down into fundamental positions that you can master on a step-by-step basis.

When children learn to read they are introduced to separate letters and sounds, which becomes a progressive method that is generally known as phonics. This method has proved time and time again to be the most effective way of teaching reading. Other methods have come and gone under the name of modern innovation but have not met the success that phonics has brought to the young reader. In a similar way, we will go through the parts of the golf swing in a way that you will master one component at a time; then we'll put them all together down the road into one great golf swing. The human mind learns in sequence and in parts. We do not learn whole things all at once in anything we attempt.

I have attended Jim McLain's Golf School at Doral Golf Resort and Spa in Miami on two occasions. The master instructors use McLain's theory of breaking the swing into eight parts and concentrating on making those moves and finding those positions as you learn. It is interesting to watch the students struggle with the positions at the beginning and then see the light come on and see significant results by the end of the week. Of course a week is not enough time to develop the swing permanently, but such a learning environment sets the stage for the learning to continue and for results to develop well into the future. It is almost like watching first-graders struggle with the sounds of letters in September and then seeing them read sentences in June. While learning, try to recognize those moments when you feel that you have just learned something or when you say, "Aha!" to yourself.

The Backswing

Golf is indeed a game of opposites: you swing down to make the ball go up; the lower you score the better you finish; and to hit the ball forward you must start the club backward. The backswing has two main purposes: it places the club in a position so it can return properly to impact with the ball by creating a path for the downswing, and it coils the body back to create and store power for the move to impact. Whenever I hear "No one ever hit a ball with a backswing," I know that the person is talking about a poor backswing that lacks good fundamentals. Some have said this about the U.S. Open champion Jim Furyk's backswing. The truth is that Jim's backswing is indeed fundamentally incorrect, as he loops the club to the outside during the take-away to the point where most players would slice the ball badly.

But Jim, after his loop, sets the club into a good position at the top and delivers the club head to impact perfectly. It is simply easier to learn the fundamentals in a correct manner so that you do not have to make in-swing adjustments. The golf swing is a difficult move to make. To learn how to swing correctly, always opt for the simple and fundamentally sound as the basis for knowledge and feel.

The Take-away

The take-away and backswing are more important to the golf swing than most golfers think. A shot can be ruined by a poor move in the first few inches of taking the club back or in the speed and sequence of the movements during the backswing.

Before we discuss the backswing in detail, it is very important to address the concepts of rhythm and tempo because these elements are the backbone of a good backswing. Rhythm is the proper flow of the body movements during the swing. It sets the movements into a logical sequence. An example of rhythm in the swing is that there should be a slight shift of the weight with your feet to the front before the club starts down toward impact. Tempo, the speed and timing of the swing, is the partner of rhythm. It relates to the speed of the body parts as the swing is executed. Swinging too fast or too slow is tempo gone bad. It is much like a dance step in which the dancer goes through the routine with everything occurring just as it should and in tune with the music.

"Too fast" means moving the downswing too fast from the top before the lower body has set itself for the move to impact. Most of us, after hitting a poor shot, have heard someone say that our backswing was too fast. Actually, after watching thousands of golfers, I have noticed that many poor golfers have backswings that are too slow. The backswing should be slow enough so that we can maintain control and hit our positions and fast enough so that we needn't lift the club back and jump at the ball as we start down toward impact. I like to think of the backswing as a sweeping motion. As I swing back, I try to feel my weight shift and my wrists cock rather than thinking about when they should occur. The speed of the backswing should be one that fits your comfort level and offers you both control and accuracy of movement. It is interesting to note that Tiger Woods seems to have a slower backswing than most touring pros (such as Nick Price). Their swings fit their personalities, and both get the job done well.

A "swing thought" is a good way to remind yourself of what you should do while learning a movement. For the backswing I use the swing thought "Sweep to the top." I like to have the feeling of a long, flowing movement that is smooth with no jerky movements or rerouting of the club during the motion. As we go through the positions, remember that they are not separate little stops on the way but little markers that you pass through in one motion. You can learn the spots or positions separately, and then integrate them into the whole.

As mentioned earlier, the take-away is the first part of the backswing. A good take-away should take the club straight away from the ball, neither inside nor outside the target line. The muscles of your left shoulder and arm pushing the club back make the take-away. The hands of course hold the club, but they should not become involved in moving the club back and away from the ball, as the hands will then tend to continue to work and snatch the club back or turn the club head as it starts back. Leave the take-away to the big arm muscles, which are easier to train so that they repeat the same movement more consistently. Let the hips turn back to allow your lower body to balance itself and create the coil needed for power.

In the take-away, try to keep the club face "looking" at the ball for about one foot as it goes back. As you turn your shoulders, the club will naturally come to the inside target line and move along the desired plane. I like to equate the take-away to a plane taking off. It should start off slow and low to the ground before it rises and gains some speed. The deliberate take-away seems to help in squaring the club for both the backswing and the downswing, which translates into great impact with the ball. If you twist or jerk the club at take-away you really have to do some compensatory contortions during the swing to get it back in place. It is always better to start right; then everything that follows is much easier.

It is always valuable to have a drill to reinforce learning and create a psychomotor link to the movement. My favorite drill to develop a good take-away is to place a tee in the ground about one foot behind the ball in a straight line back along the target line. Set up to the ball in your normal address position and then in one smooth movement let your left shoulder and arm muscles bring the club head back low and slow so that it taps the tee. Keep the face of the club square to the ball during the drill.

Repeat the drill over and over until the movement is incorporated into your golf swing. You can do this drill in your home or inside during the winter months. The key is to repeat it until it becomes automatic. This is the first little test of "how good do you want to be?" If you want to have a perfect take-away, perform this drill at least one hundred times a day for a week. Some touring professionals like this drill so much that they use it just before they start their backswings while they are playing. The Masters champion Mike Weir has incorporated the take-away drill in his pre-shot routine.

If possible, do drills with some kind of added weight in order to fire and develop the muscles involved. For the take-away drill, you might want to use a weighted club such as the Momentus (Momentus Golf). The added weight also forces you to concentrate and speeds up the learning curve. When your minds sense smoething new and different they automatically gear up to learn and respond, and we concentrate better. In neurophysiology, the study of the relationship between nervous system and body response, this is called the P-300 response. If you are used to driving an SUV and a friend lets you borrow his exotic sports car, you will drive with all of your senses heightened as you learn the play of the wheel, the acceleration, turning ability, and braking. Plug this P-300 response into learning whenever you can.

While you are learning and drilling the proper take-away, keep playing and keep practicing your whole game. Let your practice time feature a good take-away with every swing. We do not want to isolate learned movements but to build it in and make it yours as you gradually improve. You can do your drills in the morning before you play or practice and then simply take it with you to play or practice. You might even try to make the drill part of your pre-shot routine, as Mike Weir did. I tried this in my own game and it does help to build in a little rehearsal move. I think that is why you see more and more professionals copying Mike Weir and bringing drills into their pre-shot routines.

Another good way to learn the take-away is to use a mirror. Place a mirror a few feet behind the ball. Watch your club come back as you start the club away from the ball. You will see how the club reacts and how well you are performing the drill.

One key to making a smooth take-away is to keep moving a bit; never stop dead over the ball before starting back. If there is one thing that will kill a good golf swing it is tension. Tension tires out our muscles and makes them fire too fast and not produce what we want from them. Golfers who stand over the ball with the club pressed down behind it are setting themselves up to fail. As you set up, keep your grip light and the club head either moving back and forth slowly à la Mike Weir or up and down to gain a feel of it. Finally ease the club head behind the ball and start back on the take-away that you have developed from your drills. You should feel no tension—the feeling is one of having the club glide back straight from the ball in a smooth and deliberate manner.

The Midpoint

The midpoint position of the backswing is when the club is pointing straight back, parallel to but inside your target line and the toe of the club is pointing straight up toward the sky. I know that you are thinking:

"How the heck am I going to remember to do all that?" You don't have to remember it while you are swinging. You just need to know what the position looks like and how it feels. Once you know how it feels any thoughts such as where the toe of the club head is during the back-swing are completely out of conscious thought.

As you swing back, several things must happen naturally. First, your shoulders will start to turn and bring the club to the inside naturally. Second, your weight will shift to the inside of your back foot to sup-port the weight that is going back. These two things should happen as a natural response to swinging the club back and not as special things that you have to try remember to execute. Golfers create their own problems in this area when they try to fight physics. Rather com-mon faults are that they try to swing the club back with just their arms, as if the arms were separate from the shoulders, and they try to keep their weight placed the same or on the front foot as the club goes back. Players who swing with their arms and make reverse pivots are to be found on every course and driving range. Remember, you must turn your shoulders back to get the club back and to load up for power. I try to get my left shoulder behind the ball at the top of my backswing and have my right shoulder point left of the target at the finish. This is my check to see if I have made a full shoulder turn. (We will discuss the shoulder turn in depth later.) Always try to use those big muscles instead of just your arms and hands.

During the take-away you must also feel your weight shift onto the inside of your back foot as the club goes back; otherwise you will have no foundation to support the weight of the club under you. If you do not feel your weight go back, you will keep it on your front foot dur-ing the backswing. On the downswing, in the classic reverse pivot your weight shifts to your back foot. A good weight shift at the mid-point of the backswing is just the opposite: about 80 percent of your weight is loaded up on the inside of your back foot when you come to the top of your swing. Think of having nothing but air under your feet supporting you naturally. As you swing back, more air has to be forced under your back foot to maintain your balance and support.

When you start the downswing, you must slide your weight onto the front foot so that you have a platform to support your weight as you move through impact and into your finish position.

As we have stated earlier, one of the purposes of the backswing was to get the club in the proper position to deliver it back down to impact. The midpoint of the backswing is a critical checkpoint for getting the club on the right path, or swing plane. It is at this point that many golfers lose their way. If the club is pointing away from the target line or behind us, we have made a serious mistake that can be hard to correct during the swing. The best way to check to see if you are hitting this checkpoint correctly is to try this drill:

Lay a two-by-four along your target line just outside the ball so the shaft points directly at your target. Take your stance so that you are set up square to your target line. Lay two other clubs so that they are parallel to your toe line and extend back in a straight line that is parallel to your target line. Now swing back to the midpoint position. The shaft of your club should be directly over and parallel to the clubs lying along your toe line. If your club's shaft points outward or inward, you have somehow turned or twisted it too much. As a drill, repeat swinging the club to this midpoint position until you automatically have it parallel to the club on the ground.

Why is this so important? If you are off at this position, chances are that you are going to have trouble getting the club head back to square and more than likely you will hit a severe slice or hook. For example, if the club is pointing away from the target line at the midpoint, you will come down toward the ball from an outside-in path, and you will hit the ball so that it spins in a clockwise direction and create a big slice. If you point the club to the inside the opposite happens: when you come into the ball you will close the face to get it square and cause the ball to spin so that it hooks badly right to left.

Having the toe of the club pointing straight up in the air means keeping the club head square. If you placed the club face squarely behind the ball and then lifted it up straight in front of you the toe of the club would point straight up. If you tilt it right it will be open and will hit the ball to the right; if it points to the left it will be closed and will hit the ball to the left. The same thing holds true for the midpoint. Keeping the toe pointing straight up means that you are keeping the club face square and not twisting your hands or arms so that it will hit the ball left or right.

When you do your midpoint drill with the clubs or with a mirror, always check that the club face is square. Drill by swinging back to the midpoint and holding it there to check. You should have almost no thought of the take-away. Your goal is to hit your spot so that the club is parallel to the club on the ground with the toe pointing up. Repeat this drill until you can hit your mark with precision.

The Top of the Backswing

The final position of the backswing is the one at the top. In this position, your shoulders should be coiled so that the left shoulder is at least under your chin and behind the ball if possible. Your back should be completely turned away from the target. Your head either hasn't moved or has moved laterally back a bit—but never up or down.

You should feel as if your left arm is fully extended but not rigid. Your weight is now solidly on the inside of your back foot with your back knee still slightly flexed. If you straighten your back leg, there is a tendency to create a spinning move on the downswing instead of pushing off the back toward impact.

The feeling is one of being coiled back, ready to uncoil and release the stored power. Great golfers refer to this as creating torque in the swing. By limiting the amount of hip turn and increasing the amount of shoulder turn you make your body into a coiled spring. Then, when you start the downswing and go through impact you are releasing the coiled-up spring and unwinding the power that you have stored up in the backswing.

To gain this feeling of coiling and uncoiling, you need to be flexible in your upper torso. You do not want to injure your back or shoulders so you must build up your strength and flexibility. In chapter 7 we will go deeper into drills, exercises, and thoughts that will help promote flexibility and strength and prevent injury. For now, always warm up carefully by stretching and loosening your muscles before your practice or play. Do not attempt to make a big shoulder turn before your body has been conditioned to do it.

A good way to check your full backswing is to line up in front of a mirror as if it were the target. Check to see if you are lined up correctly with your feet, hips, and shoulders at address, and then watch yourself hit your positions in the backswing. When you get to the top of the backswing, see whether your back is completely turned toward the mirror and whether your club is pointing straight from behind your left shoulder. The club should never dip below parallel at that point, as you will lose power if you swing back too far and it is difficult to get it back into position. The key for accuracy is that the shaft should be pointing just left of the target and parallel to your target line. If it is pointing to the right of the target, you have "crossed the line" and have set yourself up to make a big slice swing.

Once you have swung back to the top and have the feeling of being coiled with your weight set, you have finished your backswing. If you start into the downswing before you finish the backswing, you defeat the purposes of the backswing. Finish what you start.

The Hands and Wrists

Your hands and arms must rotate back and move up as the club swings back. I prefer a simple method to accomplish this cocking up of the wrists. I like the wrist to cock up gradually until the midpoint position and then just after that position go up to a 90-degree angle and no more. While you continue to coil, the wrists are already set in the proper position so you can forget about them. Just after the midpoint position, your arms and club shaft should make an L. Hold that angle and do not allow your hands or wrists to lose control by dipping the club at the top. If you are having troubles controlling the club at the top, check your grip to see if you are holding the club correctly as we discussed (see pages 26–33).

Where to Look

One of the most common questions I get from students is how to look at the ball itself. Most good golfers tend to look at the point where the club will come in contact with the ball. Once you find a spot on the ball to look at, hold your focus there. Keeping your head still will also help you to keep focus. One player focuses on one dimple on the ball, and I tried this out, but it caused too much tension and led to the tendency to be ball-bound. One of the feelings that I want to instill is that you should swing so that it feels as if the ball just got in the way. Being fixated on the ball might lead you to try and steer the club too much.

The Effective Backswing Practice

To learn a proper backswing, you need to repeat the steps, hit your spots, and check your positions. As you practice the backswing, think these five thoughts:

1. I will make a smooth takeoff, with everything going back straight and together.

2. I will feel the left shoulder push the club back and the weight shift to my back foot.

3. I will go through the midpoint with the club pointing straight behind me and the toe up.

4. I will cock my wrists slowly to the L position and hold this position until the top.

5. At the top, I will feel loaded up on the back foot, fully coiled with my shoulders, and ready to release the power to the ball.

The Downswing

If I had to select the one point in the golf swing that separates good players from poor ones and good shots from bad, it is the instant when the backswing ends and the downswing begins. At the top of the swing common faults are made: casting (letting the wrist go), looping the club forward (the slicer's go-to move), and—the most common of all—rushing the arms and hands down before any other body parts move. This is not intended to scare you but simply to point out that the top of the swing is a critical point that must be mastered if you are to become a really solid player.

The transition from backswing to downswing does take some talent and coordination as it brings in timing and the repositioning of several body parts to effectively reverse movement and deliver power and accuracy.

To get a mental picture of what is going at this moment in the swing, let's look at what a baseball pitcher does to wind up to deliver the ball. Once the pitcher has finished his windup, his back is usually turned toward the catcher or target, his weight is on his back foot with his back knee bent, and his arm is back and ready to start forward.

1. First the pitcher pushes off from the rubber with his back leg.

2. His hips begin to unwind, and then his shoulders.

3. His arm is poised with the ball as his front foot lands, and then his arm and shoulder fire directly at the target.

4. His shoulders and hips turn to complete his follow-through and he lands in a balanced position.

This sequence of correct body movements is comparable to that of a golfer's downswing. Here are the common faults at the top of the pitch of the average golfer, expressed in terms of the baseball pitcher's delivery:

- The pitcher would throw his arm away from his body and then bring it in sharply to get it back toward the target. (The slicer)
- Once into the end of the windup, the pitcher would use just his arm and hand to throw the ball. (Most common golfer's fault)
- Instead of winding back and placing the weight on the foot on the rubber, the pitcher would start with his weight on the front foot and shift it to the back foot as he threw the ball. (The reverse pivot)

Of course, no one would be able to pitch like that, but I am not exaggerating when I use these illustrations of what golfers do in the golf swing. Perhaps this explains why 90 percent of all golfers cannot break 100 on a regulation course with their average round. Becoming a good player necessitates gaining an understanding of where a lot of swings go wrong and knowing how to make the correct movement during the transfer stage in the swing.

It cannot be overstated: before you start your downswing, you must finish your backswing. To finish your backswing, you must have turned your shoulders and hips, your weight is on the inside of your back foot, and the club is pointing parallel to the target line. You do not hold this position for very long, as it is just a fleeting moment in a total movement, but to be the player that you want to be, you must know what this moment feels like. For many players it is not a real stop but a passage. By that I mean that if you watch some of the touring professionals swing in slow motion, you will see that their backswings glide to a finish while their lower body is already moving toward shifting the weight onto the front foot. They do indeed finish their backswings but there is a little phase where the backswing is finishing while the weight transfer is beginning down below. Once the club comes to a stop, the player is ready to move to the downswing without any obvious shift as his lower body already is set to receive the weight transfer.

There is no conscious pause at the top. Some players look as though they are holding the club still for a moment, but in actuality their legs are beginning to drive. Bob Murphy of the Champions Tour looks as though he is coming to a stop at the top but actually he is shifting his weight during the pause of the club. The best way to picture this moment of transfer is to see it as a fluid motion and not a static one.

My favorite way of getting this move correct in the swing is to use a waltz timing: "And a one and a two . . ." In practice, set up over the ball. Start the take-away as you say to yourself, "And a . . ." Swing the club back with the word "one." Make the transfer and weight shift with the word "and." Swing through to impact with the word "two."

"And a one and a two" is the rhythm and timing device for your swing. Use a tempo that best fits your swing tempo and make sure that you do the things that must be done when you say the words.

Starting the Downswing

Most great golfers feel that the downswing starts with a shift of the weight from the back foot to the front foot. Older players used to plant their left heel down as a sign to themselves that they were ready to start the downswing. Modern players do not lift their left heels off of the ground, but Jack Nicklaus still uses this method of timing. You should feel a little bump in your hips as the weight gets over to your front foot while you are still holding the club back or it is gliding to a stop in your backswing. The legs begin the uncoiling that you have built up in making your backswing. As the legs turn toward the target, the uncoiling continues up to your chest and shoulders. You can feel your left shoulder turn under your chin as you start forward while your head remains in place with your eyes still focused on the ball. Think of your spine as a rod that remains in place as your hips and shoulders, then arms and hands are rotated around it.

As the right shoulder starts to come down and under your chin your arms should lag behind and your wrists still hold that L position. The lag that you are creating is like cracking a whip. The big muscles of the back and shoulders turn and the smaller parts of the body, the arms and hands, are the smaller part of the whip that makes the crack because they are being pulled so fast. This doesn't mean that you have to muscle the swing to hit it a long way. The speed of the golf swing is caused by centrifugal force and gravity. These forces create more speed and power than you can generate from your muscles. A light grip and a big turn will amplify the speed of the swing. It is interesting to note that the long-drive champions know their physics. First, most of them are very tall, which creates a big arc. Secondly, they use extra-long shafts, to take advantage of speed being built up and released by centrifugal force. Finally, they make exaggerated turns with their shoulders that are great for long-drive contests as they build tremendous coil around their spines. Unfortunately, this type of swing does not lend itself to scoring on the golf course where control is needed. It is like having an Indy car on New York City streets. Their swings do, however, serve as an extreme model of how power is created.

The move down with your hands and arms is also a critical one: letting things happen is better than trying to manipulate the move. Golfers get into trouble by trying to get their hands and arms into the swing at this point of the downswing. Usually this is where a golfer will do something to correct a fault or compensate for a poor setup position. The player who slices the ball will route his or her hands away from the body and come into the ball from outside the target line, hoping to hit the ball left so that when the ball slices it will come back to the middle of the fairway.

This is where you need to let go and get out of your own way. From the top, as you turn your shoulders, let gravity and the movement of your trunk and shoulders deliver the club head to the ball. Gravity will let your arms fall faster than you can move them on your own. Hold your wrists cocked as you start down and gravity too will release them naturally as you enter the hitting zone near the ball. The club should be traveling at its top speed at impact and just after impact without any real input or intentional manipulation from you. Let it happen. Great golfers refer to the moment of impact as having the ball get in the way of the club head as it passes through. In other words, there is no attempt to "hit" the ball. It just happens and you should not fight it. Learn to trust the club to get the ball into the air and trust your swing to deliver the ball toward your target. The club head delivers tremendous power to the ball in this tiny fraction of a second that we call impact. The club face actually turns from open to square and then closed in a 180-degree move. You should never try to hold the club face open and square to the target line after impact, as this is not possible in a good golf motion. Your right hand will come over your left but the club head should continue toward the target. All this happens so quickly that you just need to learn the basics of the swing—the impact scenario will take care of itself unless you try to introduce something else. When we discuss practice later, we will work on developing our letting-go skills and developing true trust in the club and the swing.

Impact occurs so quickly that you must rehearse the moves in slow motion to learn them and then just let it go. At impact, the feeling is one of having your hips clearing out of the way for your arms to pass through. Your right shoulder should come under your chin as you strike the ball and the club fires straight through toward the target. Your head will start to come up when your shoulder comes under your chin and moves by your head. Do not try to "keep your head down," though you may have heard this often. Holding your head in place against the forward movement will only restrict your swing. Look at stop-action photos of David Duval and Annika Sorenstam and you will see that their heads are well ahead and up from the ball at the moment of impact. I would not advise trying this, as they have developed eye-hand coordination beyond us mere mortals, but the photos do serve to point out that your head should come up to keep the flow of the swing going through impact.

One "swing thought" that I use in practice to make a full turn and make sure that my left shoulder gets under my chin and behind the ball on the backswing and then have my right shoulder come under my chin at impact is "Right shoulder under, left shoulder under." With this I signal it is okay to have my head come up as I fire through impact. You cannot have any intricate thoughts in your head about manipulating the club head through impact, so please do not try to control things that cannot be controlled! A swing thought that I liked was given by Tiger Woods about hitting his driver: as he comes into the ball he feels like he is delivering an uppercut as a boxer would throw a punch to an opponent's chin. This is a great image as it helps you feel that you are firing the right side as you strike the ball.

After impact, you should feel the club extend out toward the target naturally. This is not a stiff movement but a natural extension. When I work with Sandra Palmer, she tells me to let the club "chase" the ball after impact. The club will come to the inside naturally but you should have the feeling of the club's following the ball toward the target in order to build a powerful extension.

The Follow-Through

In the follow-through position you can see what kind of swing was made. It is the report card of golf. In the perfect follow-through position almost all of your weight is on your left foot. From your left leg to your head your body is straight up and down. Your right shoulder is pointing a little to the left of your target, your eyes are looking directly at the target, and the club grip is over your left shoulder. You can just tap the ground with your left toe. When I taught, I always called the follow-through the PGA or LPGA pose. I encouraged my students to get to the posing position as a result of their swings. When they were able to get to the pose without manipulating anything, then they had made a great swing. When I taught groups of young children, I was always amazed at how well and how fast they could learn a great follow-through position. I could simply say, "Tap your toe on the finish" and I would see ten little Tigers posing with follow-through positions.

Look at the follow-through position of your model player. Copy that position in a mirror until you have it exactly the same. Swing a club up from an imaginary ball over and over and get to that position time after time. Repeat this drill until the follow-through position is the only way that you can naturally finish your swing. You will be surprised to find that learning how the swing ends can affect how the swing happens. It may be learning in reverse, but it works.

A good follow-through will show you how balanced you are and, more important, what kind of swing path you made. If you fall forward, you are swaying into the ball with your upper body and not shifting your weight with your feet and hips. If you finish on your back foot and cannot tap your toe, you have made the dreaded reverse pivot that we discussed earlier. If your club is out in front of you or pointing to the right you have not made a good turn and have probably hit a slice or blocked shot to the right of your target. If you can, have someone videotape your swing and pay strict attention to your follow-through position. See how closely your follow-through position matches that of your model player's.

Some Thoughts on the Golf Swing

The golf swing should be made as simple and effortless as possible. It may seem that there are a lot of things to remember to do and not do, but actually if you break the swing down into components, learn them, and then put them together, the swing should become easy to acquire. I like to think of the golf swing as very similar to a dance step. Many people who have little or no athletic ability can dance pretty well. Why is it that if we place a little white ball on the ground, the same people become completely awkward trying to swing a golf club? My thought is that the white ball creates a mental reaction that causes these players to want to control every movement to help the ball get into the air, stay in the fairway, and go far as possible. All these controlling thoughts are paralyzing in nature as they cause tension and prevent the proper brain-to-body relationship that we discussed in chapter 1.

You can and will develop a great golf swing through building your knowledge base, gaining an appreciation of why certain moves are made during the swing, and, most important, gaining the feel of a great swing. When I start off very young children, I just have them hit balls to let them experience the freedom and joy of just whacking a ball with no dos or don'ts to impede their natural tendencies. Surprisingly, young children learn what works and what doesn't in a short time. Then, I hit the ball and have them watch my swing and tell them to copy what I do. I do not give any instruction at this point but simply let them be copycats. I always get a thrill and a laugh to see how well they can mimic my swing right down to my little mannerisms as I set up to the ball. It is almost as if they are making fun of me, but many of them are able to copy my swing down to a T. Then, with their new swings that they have no reason not to trust, they start to hit the ball into the air straight and true. They get so excited that they will begin to rush to hit one ball after another as fast as possible. These have been my happiest moments in teaching golf. Recently I was talking to a fellow pro who specializes in teaching kids and he said the very same thing about them before I mentioned anything about my experience.

The lesson here is to learn like a child. Open your mind to learning and be in the mode to accept ideas and change freely and without question. My worst experiences in teaching have been when a student has said "I can't" or "I won't" do something that I was trying to get across. Later we will talk about how to take a lesson, but for now, focus on being a learner. The results may not come right away—and they seldom do with golfers who have played the game for years, because a lot of unlearning has to happen. This is also tied into freeing your mind to learn new things. You may hit ground ball after ground ball for a while, but if your fundamentals are good and you start to hit your positions during the swing, eventually you will start to say, "Aha!" as the ball soars into the blue sky.

That "Aha!" moment is something that all good players have experienced at some point in their golfing lives. Mine came when I was about eight years old and a caddy. I was hitting balls on a baseball field with an older kid. He showed me some things and after a series of grounders, the ball suddenly soared into the air with no effort and I was hooked on golf for life. My sincere hope is that this book will give you that moment, regardless of the level of play you are at right now.

As you go about building a great golf swing, learn your positions by studying your model player and then copy the positions in a full-length mirror. Place these positions in your memory in a way that has to do with feel, not any mental exercise or conscious thought. Rehearse the separate swing positions at home or in your backyard, using a mirror. Once you get to the range, rehearse the positions a few times before going into a full swing.

Certainly you should commit yourself to becoming a good golfer through hard work and practice as well as open learning, but you need to understand that the swing itself is not improved by "trying too hard." By that I mean the golf swing is a rhythmic movement that is flowing and smooth and that is consistent, essentially the same every time. "Trying too hard" is hitting at the ball, swinging hard, and trying to lift it into the air, hoping for the best but expecting the worst. Stop trying.

The most important part of hitting golf shots that fly far and straight is good contact. When we swing faster than we can handle, we enter an area our minds are not adjusted to. We should swing at a tempo that produces solid contact on a regular basis. My tempo is relatively slow, but solid contact allows me to hit the ball long enough to play any course that I want. I am okay with this and accept my distance from the tee and with my irons, as I can still make good scores. I feel a lot is being missed by those who think golf is all about hitting long drives. You do not get points for the distance you hit a ball or the iron you used to hit it onto the green. Men seem to get hung up on hitting the ball a long way while losing sight of scoring and keeping the ball in play. Women do not seem to have ego problems around hitting a ball farther than their playing partners. For men, though, it is a source of pride and for razzing others, which is okay for fun.

I concentrate on swinging in balance and having my swing look great. If it looks great, chances are that I am hitting my swing positions and hitting good shots. Often when I am hitting balls at a driving range, people come over to ask whether I am a pro, not because I am hitting balls over the fence but because my swing is smooth and graceful—golfers who know the game call it a "good action," and they know a good action when they see one. One time I was playing a casual round when I saw a player about three fairways over make a wonderful swing. He had that special action that you just do not see very often. I asked a playing partner who he was. The answer came that he was a former touring pro. Bingo!

Take pride in your swing. Make it smooth and powerful, and hold that PGA or LPGA Tour finish after each shot, good or bad. When I talk to myself, I simply say, "Make the best swing possible." By that I mean that I will sweep the club back while making a big shoulder turn, I will feel my weight shift forward, and I will uncoil into impact.

I will let the club chase the ball and finish like a touring pro with a great pose.

This is all done with feel. The mind and body just hit the positions and the swing grows out of the hours of practicing the elements that we have been learning. No conscious thought intrudes except for a little word of encouragement such as the sentence above to remind me to make the best possible swing that I can. You cannot ask anymore from yourself if you have worked diligently at home and in practice.

All individuals who are successful in a particular area have the true confidence that comes from knowing that they are good at what they do. These people do not have to tell others how good they are. Their performance does all the talking and provides all the publicity they need. The best feeling in golf and in life is knowing each day that you are trying your best and that the good things that happen are a result of your effort. Golf can teach you a lot about yourself. How well are you willing to learn? How do you feel about yourself and about doing well? Do you feel confident in trusting yourself? How important is it to you to do something right? The same things that can make you a good golfer can help make you a good mother or father or a good person. Golf is not nearly as important as life matters but it is a component in your life that enriches and enhances your life. If you are going to spend a good deal of time at the game—why not be good at it?

As we are going through learning the "how" of learning the game, pause and remind yourself that this is enjoyment and not work. If golf starts to feel like work or if you play because you think you have to, it really is not recreation. As you become better and even good at the game your enjoyment and sense of accomplishment should transcend your attitude and your growth within the game will continue to motivate and enrich you.

I tried playing tennis several times. I found that I could learn the fundamentals well but I never could develop an appreciation for the game. Thousands love the game and enjoy it, but I was not comfortable playing in a box and relying on what someone else did more than what I could control myself. I knew very early on that this was not a sport for me because my appreciative component would never allow me to learn—my motivation to excel in the game simply would not be there. I think that starting out as a caddy was the beginning of my love affair with golf. Things might have been different if I had started as a ball boy in tennis. My point is that as we go through this learning phase, try to keep your motivation level up and visualize yourself as a great golfer playing better than you have ever imagined. Learn to love the game. This is a very real possibility and is within your reach.

The Clubs

Golf clubs are the tools of the trade. You need to have the right equipment, and that does not necessarily mean the most expensive. The clubs should suit you in the way they sit behind the ball, lie flat on the ground, and send the ball into flight. Clubs that fit you will do all of the above without your bending over or standing awkwardly at any time. Standard clubs fit most people. Always try out demonstration clubs before you buy. Have a professional watch you swing and assist you in your purchase. The ball flight can be adjusted by the type of shaft chosen. Many stores offer fitting systems and can measure your swing speed to best meet your specifications. There are two basic groups, irons and woods, and two subgroups, putters and wedges.

The Driver

The main purpose of the driver is to get the ball out as far and straight as possible. The driver strikes fear into the hearts of more golfers than any other club, for two reasons: it has less loft than any other club, and it has the longest shaft. I have seen many players use a three-wood from the tee and simply give up on the driver as too hard to use, but good players use their driver and putter more than any other clubs on a regular basis. If you leave your driver in the trunk of your car, you will miss the benefits it can provide.

The Shaft

One of the first considerations in selecting a driver is the shaft. A driver's shaft flexes more than that of any other club. The flex, or "kick," is the motion the shaft makes as it moves toward impact. The flex should match your swing speed—the speed of the club as it goes through impact. Slower speed requires greater flex. Men tend to play with shafts that are too stiff, as they see all the touring professionals using them. But touring professionals' swing speeds range from 110 up to 130 mph. Few of us can match those speeds—nor would we attempt to swing that fast in the first place. Basically, shafts are rated for four levels of flex:

Flexible (A): Good for those (seniors, juniors, and many women) whose swing speed is below 80 mph and who rely on a smooth, flowing swing to make contact.

Regular (R): This shaft is moderately stiff. The regular shaft fits the swing speed of players who swing in the 80 to 90 mph range—about 80 percent of all golfers.

Stiff (S): The stiff shaft is made for players who have a swing speed greater than 90 mph. This shaft is best for strong players who have great acceleration at impact.

Extra stiff (X): The extra-stiff shaft is for the most powerful hitters. This shaft is found on the PGA Tour but seldom at your local club. Unless you can swing at touring-pro speeds forget the X shaft. I tried to hit a touring pro's driver that had a 7-degree loft and an X shaft and all I could do was hit low-line drives about 100 hundred yards.

Most drivers today come with shafts that are about 45 inches long for men's clubs and about 42 inches long for women's. Manufacturers have made the shafts longer in recent years to create a wider and longer arc, which helps build club-head speed and momentum. You should feel comfortable holding the club about six inches from your body and having it sit nicely behind the ball. If you are very tall you may need extra-long clubs, but tall people usually have long arms, so get the feel of a normal-length club first. Shorter people may require a flatter lie on their clubs.

The Driver's Head

Swing the the driver and get a feel for how it flows. It should have some weight to it as you need this for speed. You may think that you can swing a light driver faster, but you will be sacrificing accuracy, as the ball will easily fly off in the wrong direction. New drivers have large heads of up to and over 400 cubic centimeters (cc), but they still feel light, as they are filled with lightweight materials or are hollow. The use of titanium has allowed club makers to balance the driver with heel and toe weighting and to create a lightweight and hard face for good impact.

Hitting the Driver

As you begin to transform your game, you will become a steady player off of the tee. A tee shot in the fairway is a major advantage for scoring when measured against drives in the rough or, worse, in the woods. The top money winners on the Tour usually hit a lot of fairways. Vijay Singh and Fred Funk are two players who hit a lot of fairways and consistently place well in the money rankings.

As you begin to learn the driver in order to become a great player, eliminate any tendencies that may have sabotaged you in the past. Teaching and watching many players over the years has shown me that the following mistakes seem to be the most common culprits responsible for poor tee shots:

- Teeing the ball too low
- Poor ball position
- Overswinging
- Fear

Tee it high and let it fly. Often, average golfers tee the driver so low that they pre-set the contact point to the bottom of the driver. The bottom of the driver's face has almost no loft and will produce a low shot. Low shots tend to slice or hook very easily. The driver is actually the one club in which you contact the ball with a slight upward movement instead of hitting down on the ball. Your swing thought is to sweep the ball off the tee. With the new large-head drivers, tee the ball high enough so that the ball sits just above the club head when you place the head directly behind it. When you set up to hit your drive, check the height every time and change or adjust the height if it is not perfect.

We spoke about ball positioning earlier; it is never more important than with the driver. If you have the ball too far back or too far forward, these mistakes are magnified by shot dispersion. A ball that is placed too far back in your stance will cause you to hit the ball to the right. A ball that is placed too far forward will result in pop-up shots or pulled ones that fly well left of your target. If you are hitting your drives well and they travel a good distance, but they are flying left or right, they can often be corrected by checking your ball position.

Find a good practice area to experiment with your ball position with your driver. First, set up to the ball with your feet together. Turn your front foot a little open (toward your target). Line up the ball opposite your left instep and then move your right foot back until it is under your right shoulder. Take your normal swing and check your ball flight and direction. The ball should fly like a plane taking off—gradually rise to a point—and then start down while still traveling forward. Drives that start low and zoom up quickly or ones that start low or high and stay that way are telling you that your ball position is off for you. Try moving the ball a little forward or a little back in slight increments while going through the feet-together routine to get a good measurement. You should experiment until you find the ball flight that gives you the best results. It is a good sign if your ball draws or fades slightly—you have found your ideal ball position. Nasty slices or hooks will need further work to correct and may not be the fault of ball positioning alone. When you go to the course, place your feet together to make sure you have the same ball position every time. After a while you will recognize this position from feel and your body's natural setup. Until then, use the routine to help bring what you learned on the range to the course.

As you set up to your drive, your hands should be slightly behind the ball and in no way forward of it. Your head should naturally be behind the ball; your eyes move to look at its back. Tilt your spine slightly toward your back foot. This little tilt helps your swing path and balance to accommodate the long shaft. It will also give you the feeling of being behind the ball and then moving into it at impact. The left shoulder is higher than the right, but not stiff or raised artificially. Some touring professionals have told me that they place a little more weight on their back foot at address with the driver in order to help with a weight shift without swaying. This is a good idea to pre-set your weight—since it has to go back anyway, why not put it there to start? Keep your knees flexed and feeling soft so your legs can move freely. Stand about an inch wider than normal.

Once we get a driver in our hands, we tend to think of one thing: smacking the ball as far as possible. Remember this one adage: swinging hard does not equate to longer distance. Once you accept that distance comes from a coordinated swing that generates speed from centrifugal force and contact with the center of the club face, you are on the road to learning to hit great drives. Tiger Woods's swing speed is 130 mph, but his backswing is smooth and unhurried. His speed is generated from the tremendous turn and acceleration of his shoulders, which whip his arms through the ball. Few of us will ever approach Tiger's movement, but we can copy the essentials of a well-timed swing that delivers our maximum swing speed at impact.

To hit a long drive, think slow instead of fast. Take the club back low and slow and straight back from the ball. Feel your shoulder push the club back and keep your hands and wrists soft as the backswing takes place. The driver swing features a full backswing in which your shoulders turn so much that you should feel that your left shoulder is behind the ball when you reach the top of your backswing. Your back will be completely turned to the target but your head remains in place with your eyes on the ball. The downswing starts with the shift in the weight of your lower body, starting with your feet. Be patient. Let your legs clear, hips open, and shoulders unwind, and let them pull your arms and hands through impact and up to a great finish. At no time should you feel that you are exerting force while making the driver swing. Hold the club lightly and let the uncoiling bring you the speed you need. Feel the club head chase the ball after impact and watch it fly long and true.

Probably the most important factor is removing fear and building trust. The driver is designed to lift the ball into the air and hit it straight and far, so you do not have to make many manipulations to achieve success with the long club. One thing that you must do is trust the club to do its job.

On the practice tee, select two flags or two trees to simulate a fairway. This gap becomes your target. Your goal is to get all of your drives on the fairway. Never go to the practice area and smack drives without any sense of direction. When you get to the course, you will have no confidence in hitting a tight fairway because your mind has learned to smash the ball in any direction as the correct way to hit a driver. You must retrain yourself to think of the driver as accurate—one club that you can consistently count on to get you onto the short grass.

Once you set up to your imaginary fairway, start from behind your ball and go through your pre-shot routine with every shot. When you step up to the ball, place your feet together to set your ball position. You are training yourself to pay attention to the fundamentals, which will make you a confident player. That guy several yards away who is spraying the balls five miles in every direction one after the other is not really learning a thing. Your practice time is a special learning time, so make every minute count. Later on we will discuss practice in detail. I want to emphasize the driver practice at this point because the driver is a tool that golfers misuse and thus never become confident with. Each time you swing, start at a speed that gets you into the "fairway" every time with a minimum of effort. Gradually increase the length of your swing, the amount of your turn, and the speed of your swing until you can gain considerable distance and still hit the fairway on the practice range. Once you start to swing at a speed that puts you off the fairway, go back to your ideal swing speed. Remember: Always take accuracy over distance!

The Fairway Woods

Fairway woods are used to hit the ball a long way from a lie in the fairway or light rough. More and more, fairway woods and utility woods are becoming popular for golfers at all levels. Annika Sorenstam does not carry any iron longer than a five-iron, but loads up on fairway woods and utility woods. Touring pros are now hitting five-woods and mid-woods, though a few years ago this was unthinkable. The reason is that fairway woods and the new utility woods are much easier to hit a long way than the long irons such as a two-, three-, or four-iron. With the new woods it is also easier to get the ball up and out of rough. The metal woods are perimeter-weighted for accuracy and have soles that glide off the fairway or through rough. They have the loft to get the ball up into the air and the mass to hit it a long way. The long irons require a great deal of skill and power. They are difficult to hit from the rough as the hosel (the part of the club head that connects with the shaft) will tangle in the grass and the loft is not high enough to get the ball up quickly.

Club configuration—your choice and selection of clubs—is an individual thing. You can carry 14 clubs and configure your selection any way that you want. But why carry a two- or three-iron if you never use it when you can carry a club that will hit the ball a long way from the fairway or get you out of trouble from the rough? Women were first to configure their bags differently, eliminating irons, and Annika led the way. Men are still reluctant to as some think hitting a utility wood instead of a two-iron shows that they lack skill or power. My own club configuration is very unconventional. I carry only the five- through nine-irons and have four wedges, three fairway woods, a driver, and a putter. The bottom line is that you have a set of clubs that will work for you and that you will use each club with confidence and for a specific reason.

The setup for the fairway woods is similar to that of the driver: the ball position is back toward your left heel or slightly behind it. With the five-wood or higher, you will move the ball commensurately farther back in your stance.

The key to hitting the fairway woods is first to resist the mistakes that almost all average golfers instinctively make: they swing too hard because they feel that they need to power it for distance, and then they try to help the ball into the air. The fairway and utility woods are made with two things in mind: hit the ball a good distance and get the ball into the air easily. In other words, let the club do what it is designed to do. Again, develop trust through practice and experience. The key is to make a smooth, unhurried swing that makes solid contact and lets the club take over from there.

The fairway wood should be swung so that you take a tiny divot, or scrapes the grass, in front of the ball. This helps you to get the lift that you want and removes any thought of trying to scoop the ball into the air. The fairway woods are also great for controlling distances and the flight of the ball with a few adjustments. You can control the distance by choking down a bit on the club, which will hit the ball shorter but still deliver the distance that you need. For example, you have the choice of hitting a choked-down five-wood easily rather than swinging hard at a four-iron. When you are hitting a fairway wood into a green, you can make the ball fly high and land soft by opening the face a little and aiming left of your target with your alignment. The ball will travel a long way, fly high, fade onto the green, and land softly. This is a great shot to learn and have in your repertoire.

Other uses of the fairway woods that are seen more and more on the tours: running the ball up onto the green when there is no bunker in front; hitting the woods from the tee anytime there is a narrow fairway or trouble ahead; even chipping with the woods from greenside rough. In the strategy section we will discuss these shots and show you how you can learn them easily.

The Irons

Your irons are the accuracy instruments of your arsenal. They are designed to hit the ball to a specific point. The ideal iron shot flies high and lands soft on the green. You do not want an iron shot to hit and bounce a long way as it lands.

Play the long irons (two- through four-iron) toward your front, or just under your armpit. This allows you to accommodate for the longer shafts and contact the ball with a shallow divot, which allows the club face to get the ball into the air. With the longer irons, you should have a feeling of making a long, slow swing that gathers speed just at impact and sweeps the ball from the turf. Avoid hitting these irons from the rough, as the loft of these clubs make it difficult to get the ball up and out while powering through heavy grass. In the rough, opt for a fairway wood instead. As I mentioned above, I took the long irons out of my bag and replaced them with utility woods, which are much easier to hit and give you the same distance.

Hitting the five-iron through pitching wedge accurately is the result of proper alignment, swing plane, and the way you make contact. I have had the opportunity to watch the touring professionals practice hitting their irons up close. The thing that struck me like a bolt of lightning was that they do not hit their iron shots as the rest of us mere mortals do. The very best players hit their irons with an exaggerated downward path that hits down on the ball and enters the turf well (relatively) in front of the ball. This move into the ball creates a pinching action in which the ball is hit downward, creating a great amount of spin. The spin makes the ball fly high and the power of the swing makes it fly the desired distance. I was amazed at how hard they hit down on the ball, as if they were causing the ball to explode from the ground. The club makes contact with the ball on its way down and then a divot is taken in front of the ball when the club reaches its lowest point.

To make this swing, keep all of your fundamentals in place. Your stance becomes narrower as the club becomes shorter. Place the ball toward the middle or just left of middle of your stance. As you swing back, let your wrists cock up naturally, even though this will seem a lot earlier than with your woods or long irons. Make the L with your left arm and club pointing up into the sky as you approach the top of your swing. Because the shaft is shorter, you will not swing back to parallel at the top. You should feel loaded up with your weight on the inside of your back foot, your shoulders turned to a coiled position, and your head poised over the ball. The shift to the front started by your feet and legs happens faster than with the longer clubs as the swing's arc is much shorter. Your narrower stance and shorter backswing should help you make the weight transfer efficiently. Once you set yourself on your front foot you are almost simultaneously starting to move the club head downward.

Try to hold your wrist position—the L—in place as you move down toward impact, as this will give you that late release that creates tremendous centrifugal force through impact. Hit down at the ball and let your hand release naturally as you make contact, take a good divot, and keep your hands driving through impact. Avoid quitting at this critical moment by trying to hit at the ball or, worse, trying to lift it into the air. Feel as if you are pinching the ball out of the ground. Keep your hands moving through the impact zone and let your right shoulder come under your chin and bring you to a great finish with your weight balanced on your left side while you stand straight.

When you first practice this way of hitting your irons, make sure you are on grass and not a mat, as you could injure your hands or wrists. Make up your mind to overdo the downward path of the club so that you feel that pinching motion as you hit the ball. Do not close the club face when you hit down, as this will take the loft out of it. Keep your hands neutral so that they are not twisted left or right but simply poised to release at impact. Get the feeling of driving down at the ball and feeling your right shoulder, arms, and hands deliver the club head through the ball. Keep the shoulder passing under your chin and firing toward the target. By overdoing this movement you will experience what the pros feel in hitting down on the ball to make it spin up and out of the turf. Don't be afraid to try this, as once you experience the pinching sensation and watch the ball fly high and far you will get the "Aha!" reaction, and great iron play will be yours forever.

With the eight- and nine-irons, it may be a good idea to open your stance slightly in order to clear your hips out of the way in the short time that the swing takes. You should not overdo opening the stance but experiment on the range to see what is comfortable for you and to make sure that you can still deliver the ball on target.

Whenever I have a seven-, eight-, or nine-iron shot into a green, I get a feeling of anticipation. I have become aware of this feeling and make an effort to calm myself down before I start my routine. The feeling comes from visualizing a shot that is struck well as my club strikes the ball and takes a good-sized divot, and the ball flies high and straight and lands near the pin and then spins back a little. It's this visualization that pumps me up to perform well, guides my thinking to expect the best, and programs my mind to direct my body do what it has to do to produce the shot that I have already seen. The mind-body relationship is what all the great players have and I cannot overemphasize its importance. Once I learned it for myself, my game and focus changed dramatically. Be sure to calm that "kid in a candy store" feeling once you start to get precise with these irons.

These irons are tools for accuracy, and you must make sure that you are setting up for success. Let's look at some pointers for setting up for short irons to hit them with accuracy:

- Stand behind the ball and draw the white target line from the pin back to your ball. Select a spot (divot, leaf, spot) along your target line and a few feet in front of your ball. Keep the interim spot in your sight and look up to your target from there as you walk up to your ball. This gives you a great sense of the direction that you want your ball to take. Bunkers, water, or hazards will seem to disappear.
- Step up to the ball with your back foot first. Make sure that it is perpendicular to your target line. Next, place the club face

behind the ball so that you can see that the bottom groove of the iron is pointing directly at your interim target spot. Move your left foot in without moving the club and square your shoulders, hips, and knees to the line created by the placement of your back foot and the direction that the club face is pointing. Avoid opening or manipulating the club face at this point, as you have already placed the club in a dead aimed position much as you would do with a rifle.

- Set your hands so that they are in front of the ball at address. This will promote a swing that hits the ball with a descending blow. Place a little more weight on the front foot to avoid overshifting on your way back and failing to get to your front side first on the downswing. From the top of the swing, you want to feel well planted on your front side so it serves to pull the club down and through.

- Hold the wrists in the cocked position to the last moment. Then, at impact, there is a feeling of the wrists releasing with great speed into the ball. It is almost a feeling of snapping the hands through at impact.

- A balanced finish lets you know that you transferred your weight properly, and you can watch the flight of the ball as it soars to the target.

Selecting Your Irons

Manufacturers have engineered irons to play well in that they are forgiving for bad-contact hits and they handle the grass better as the club glides through it. You should opt for clubs that are perimeter-weighted to give yourself forgiveness and better contact on a consistent basis. Touring professionals are eschewing their blade models for perimeter-weighted clubs more and more as they are much easier to hit and becoming more and more aesthetically pleasing to look at address. Most irons now feature slightly wider soles that help the club enter and exit the ground. The older blade models tended to find resistance in the turf and required a strong swing to move through impact correctly. Graphite shafts offer better feel of the club head and a lighter overall club weight.

This chapter has given you some background knowledge, insights into the appreciative realm of the golf swing, and an introduction to building a mind-body relationship to help connect your psychomotor system to your golf swing. There is a lot to learn so take it in steps. Good learning occurs in small increments; small portions of what is to be learned are mastered before moving on, a process educators and psychologist refer to as "chunking." Master one step at a time and build on successes. Bad shots and bad rounds will happen on the way to improving. Kids fall off their bikes while learning to ride, and you too must take your lumps on your road to great golf. Be patient and let it happen by keeping a positive framework in your mind and keeping your eyes on the goals ahead.

CHAPTER THREE

The Art of Practice

I ENTITLED THIS CHAPTER AS THE "ART" OF PRACTICE TO CONVEY THAT THIS aspect of learning should not be approached as science, or drudgery. Gaining understanding of what you do in practice has a purpose and is also a vital part of the love and enjoyment of the game. Practice is something that you will *want* to do, not something you *have* to do. Surprisingly, most players never practice except for a little putting and chipping. The vast majority of those who do go to the practice or driving range do so with no clear plan in mind.

In my affective mode of the game of golf, I look at practice as recreation, enjoyment, part of the game, and the workshop in which to learn skills to become a better player. In researching this book, I asked many players why they do not practice. Even some good players said that they would rather spend their time playing on the course or doing something else or that they found practice boring. Good golfers usually look at practice in another light. They see practice as the necessary element to produce good results on the course. There is an old saying about being lucky on the golf course. Great players always respond that the more they practice, the luckier they get. If you look at the greatest athletes in all sports you will find that they did not just appear and begin to be great. Sometimes actors and singers just have that ability to begin great and then excel with coaching and practice. Great athletes are usually born with good eye-hand coordination and physical ability. In sports, however, and golf in particular, skills must be honed by practice of an amount and quality that certainly would surpass those of most other sports.

In golf, unlike so many other sports, size does not matter. Most of us could never play pro football, basketball, or soccer because of the physical ability and muscularity required. In golf, we see 100-pound young women on the LPGA smash drives farther than six-foot, 200-pound athletes in other sports, and do so with ease. Golf has a mystical character about it that combines coordination and timing with mental acumen, awareness, and creativity; this sets it apart from all other games. I would think that football, hockey, and basketball practices would become work very quickly and players would see practice as a necessary evil or negative experience. In golf, the opposite is true.

Practicing golf is an experience in freedom and creativity. It is a place and time to not only learn but to explore the secrets of the games and thrill to the moments when we hit the perfect shot or, better, when we experience an "Aha!" On the course we need to restrict our play to the shot in front of us and make sure we focus on that one task. On the practice tee, we can hit the same shot over and over while making little changes that add to our learning or increase our skill level. We can imagine shots so that any golf course or golf hole becomes ours to play. Our minds are free to call the shots and play where and how we want. In practice you can flop a shot over a bunker on the 12th hole at Augusta or try to hit a three-wood to the 18th at Pebble Beach. All you need is your visualization skills and your golf swing. You can play a round at your home course, hole by hole and shot by shot, if you want to. You can play an 18-hole round in about half an hour and enjoy it as if you were on the course itself. This is one of my favorite techniques.

Most of all, practice builds our skills. In an ascending hierarchy of benefits, practice makes us a better golfer, gives us confidence needed to hit the shots on the course, raises our self-esteem as golfers, increases our appreciation and love of the game, and enriches our lives because it makes our recreation time pleasant and rewarding. Try to make practice into play. You are not "working" on your game, since you are increasing your skills and abilities to play the game both in practice and on the course.

Develop a Plan for Practice

There are different kinds and purposes for practice. Before you set out for the range, you should have a clear idea of your goal for that day's practice session. For a pre-round warm-up you might simply work through your bag, starting with a sand wedge and finishing with the driver. But this is not a good plan for practicing to improve.

There are two principal ways to find out what and how you should practice to get better. The first way is to take a lesson from a pro and ask him or her for drills and a practice routine that you can use to work on specific elements of your swing or a particular area where you need improvement.

The second way is to take an inventory. Keep a record of about five rounds, charting for each hole distance and accuracy with your driver, greens hit and missed, and where and why. Count how many up-and-downs, sand saves, and putts you make. Every touring pro knows exactly what his or her percentages are for all categories of statistics that track their performance. If you are a good putter but hit weak or wild drives, your focus should be on developing driving skills at a greater percentage than putting. Make a list in a loose-leaf binder or input the data into a computer and make notes on how you did on the following:

- Tee shot: Number of fairways hit, distance, and position on fairway.
- Fairway woods, utility woods, or long irons: Note accuracy, distance, control, and confidence.
- Short irons: Note accuracy, impact, ball flight, and action on the green.
- Sand shots: Number of sand saves, types of lies and results, types of sand and results, fairway bunker results.
- Wedges: Accuracy to target, distance control, action on ball as it landed.
- Pitching and chipping: Accuracy, types of lies and angles and results, confidence levels, when successful and when things went wrong.

- Putting: Number of putts per round, number of par putts and number of birdie putts, three-putts and causes, reason why putts missed (left, right, short, too hard, misread, mis-hit).
- Mental considerations: Positive or negative thoughts flowing before a shot, focus on target or trouble, self-talk (positive or negative), course-strategic decisions, thoughts and feelings during pre-shot routine, club selection, awareness of elements, overall mental framework.

Be honest and thorough in your personal inventory. The data that you collect should be reflective of how you actually played and managed yourself during those rounds. The data are for your eyes only, so there is no need to hedge or embellish anything. These data will help you to structure your practice, seek instruction, and become the player that you want to be. If you can identify a weak point that results in higher scores round after round, tackle the problem directly instead of hoping that it will improve on its own by some miracle.

I visit a store quite often where one of the employees is an avid golfer and knows that I am a pro. Every time I go to this store he tells me about his game, but he always complains that he can't hit his irons well and says that if he could be a better iron player, he could be playing in the 70s. He never takes a lesson (doesn't think that they would help) and tunes out when I offer him some drills to help with iron play. I do not think my friend is very different from most men who play the game. They want to play better and simply hope that the next time they play, they will find the key to success and everything will be okay after that.

To this man I would say: Schedule a practice session with a professional. The pro should not be analyzing your swing but simply giving you drills and checking your fundamentals as you practice and hit shots. I have taken many practice lessons and find that they lead to quick improvement. Make sure you tell the pro what you want in a practice lesson: drills, routines, alignment and posture checks, etc. The pro becomes more of a coach than an instructor in this situation.

I would also counsel my friend at the store to practice as close to the situations he will find on the course. Unless you are working on a new swing move where you should just tee the ball up a little so the learning is easier, try to simulate playing conditions. The better play conditions are simulated, the better the results in making the transfer from the practice range to the golf course. In almost every other sport, players practice on the same playing field, court, or area in which they will perform. Golf is the one sport that does not offer this option readily. To see how important having the same conditions in practice is, I recently visited the Boston Celtics' practice facility in Waltham, Massachusetts. The practice court is identical to the court that they play games on at the Fleet Center in Boston. They have replicated the parquet floor, the championship banners, the lighting system, the sounds of the horns and buzzers—every detail. The players are imbued with the feel of the surroundings as they practice.

So how can you accomplish this is golf? An example is the shot from a fairway bunker. Two things always come to mind about the fairway bunker shot: first, you seldom see anyone who can hit good shots consistently from one, and second, you never see anyone practice them. Chances are, you are going to land in a fairway bunker and you will feel that you are in an unfamiliar place unless you know how to play the shot and are familiar with the shot concept. I have watched the average player open his stance, dig his feet, and open his club as if he were hitting a bunker shot from around the green, only with a longer club. The result is usually a swing that sticks the club into the sand behind the ball or weakly pops the ball out a few yards. At a PGA Tour event, I watched the very best go to practice bunkers and hit different clubs from the sand, to develop their skills and test the sand as well.

To hit a good fairway bunker shot, select a club that would be one club more than you would usually use for that distance. Set your feet into the sand only about an inch and flare your feet so that the inner parts of your shoes are deeper than the outside parts. This stance will brace you while you swing.

Choke down on the handle or grip about one inch. Swing the club while keeping your lower body still while moving only your shoulders and arms. Strike the ball cleanly without touching the sand or digging down as you would do to take a divot. The club head should catch the ball and sweep it off the sand.

The better you learn to overcome adversity the easier it is to manage shots that are on great lies. Practice the hard and master the easy. For the golfer, this means hitting balls from bad lies, out of divots, from downhill and side-hill lies, and in windy conditions. Hit shots from bunkers with bad lies in the sand, hit flop shots over bunkers, and chip from heavy rough. Search for a practice facility that will offer you options to practice dealing with those challenges. Here are some more ideas for effective and enjoyable practice:

- Build a practice station at your driving range. Set clubs on the ground as described earlier to find ball position and alignment. Bring dowels, aiming rods, swing trainers, or chalk or lime to build lines and devise drills to enhance your station. You might keep all your practice equipment in a separate bag that you take with you each time you go to the range.
- Compete with a friend. Have competitions to see who can hit the ball closer to a target or make a sand shot or two putts from long distance. The competition will raise your awareness of what you are doing and will actually place you in a pressure situation that better simulates how you feel on the course than practice alone.
- Play a practice round on your course. Find a time when your course is empty or few people are playing, such as very early on a weekday morning or later in the day. Go out by yourself and play two balls. You might play one ball aggressively and one conservatively to see which type of approach fits your game. Hit from trouble spots such as deep rough, near hazards, out of sand, and over water. This practice will build confidence and remove fear and is also a good opportunity to practice shots from various slopes.
- Gather a list of drills. Using knowledge from reading, your pro, or from videos, make a list of drills you can use to perfect and instill the proper movement or feel that you are trying to develop. (Later in this chapter we will go over some great drills to use in practice.)

- Write out one specific goal for each practice round and stick to it.
- Rehearse the fundamentals. Plan that every practice shot requires you to rehearse the fundamentals—grip, stance, posture—every time you set up to a ball.
- Pace your practice. Have a drink of water, eat snacks, and generally pace your practice. Stop practicing when you start to feel tired or something starts to feel sore. Listen to your body, as practicing while tired or injured is not productive practice.

Create a plan that will hone in on the areas that you need to work on to improve your game. Let's say your wedge game is hurting you because although you hit the green most of the time, often you are too far from the hole to make birdie or par. The first thing you need to do is plan your practice.

- Write your goal down. "Hit wedges closer to the pin with accuracy."
- Detail steps to accomplish the goal. "I will use dowels to help with alignment; practice with the pitching wedge, sand wedge, and lob wedge only and not bring any other club to the range; check my ball position and fundamentals on every shot."
- Identify flaws to correct. "Ball flight too low, ball flies to the right of the target, contact is not solid," etc.
- List correction techniques. "Check alignment of body to the target from behind the ball after setting up and laying down the dowels; check ball position; note where ball is being struck on the club face; see how swing changes such as shoulder turn and weight shift affect ball flight."

Once you have a general plan, list the drills to work on that day. In the previous example your list might look like this:

- Stop club half way back and parallel to the ground to see if the club is on plane. Drill by starting the club from this position and going into the swing from there.

- Place an aiming rod on the ground about 10 yards away on my target line and start by hitting balls over the rod.
- Take practice swings with my eyes closed before hitting the ball. (This drill is to develop a physical feel for the force that will produce proper distance.)

After you list the drills you will do, creative a practice sequence to follow:

1. Stretch and loosen muscles, hands, and arms.

2. Swing two clubs together slowly and rhythmically in half swings.

3. Hit some sand wedge shots with short swings. The aim is to hit each ball squarely on the face to build eye-hand coordination for the day.

4. Select a target about 25 yards away and start with the lob wedge. Place practice station with dowels for alignment and ball position. Place a rod 10 yards into the ground along the target line.

5. Go through pre-shot routine by starting from behind the ball and sighting to the target. Walk up to the ball while looking at the target and back to the ball. Step into the hitting station and check fundamentals. Swing and aim so that the ball passes over the aiming rod and lands near the target. If the shot was not good, go back and check ball position and alignment as well as fundamentals. Start over.

6. Repeat routine and hitting shots until a high majority of shots have a good ball flight and land near the target.

7. Select a new target that is 50 yards away. Go through the same setup of building a station and setting an aiming rod.

8. Hit your sand wedge to this target by choking down on the handle and making short, crisp swings. If ball is off target, start from a position that has your club pointing straight back and along your toe line. Lift the club to the cocked position and swing through. If this corrects the problem, make normal swings until most shots have the ball flight and land near the target.

9. Select targets of gradually increasing length until you are hitting full pitching wedge shots.

10. Walk yourself back by returning gradually to shorter targets until you are back to the 25-yard one. Move back only after achieving the results that you want.

This may seem a little tedious to you when you read it on paper. In actuality, you will get a great deal of enjoyment and satisfaction from practicing in a methodical way that produces noticeable results. You will gain in confidence and self-esteem. The next time you go to play on your course, that self-esteem and confidence will be there to help produce the shot you want. When you start to hit your wedges close and make those birdie and par putts, the practice time will have paid off in dividends. When you come to a wedge shot you will not fear it, have self-doubts, or lack confidence in your ability to pull it off. You will not have to labor on the course with thoughts of mechanics and manipulations, as your mind and body have been set up for success from your practice. All you have to do now is to set up to the ball and trust your swing with a feeling of inner confidence that will translate into success.

One of the key elements to developing your game is to practice with creativity. Our minds have incredible abilities beyond our present comprehension. We do know that we learn and acquire knowledge and skills throughout our lifetimes and the brain can adapt to both learning and implementing learning. Being creative in practice means getting away from the drudgery of learning that is not always effective. For example, a history class where children read one paragraph at a time about Native Americans is very limited. Having Native American speakers, visiting museums or tribal lands, handling artifacts, engaging in rituals, and eating foods from the people themselves is creative learning that stimulates the mind.

Similarly, hitting wedge shots of different lengths and varying the order that we hit them in causes the brain to fire signals to adjust the backswing and downswing to the changing stimuli. This is creative learning, unlike hitting a thousand pitching wedges one after the other with a full swing.

Going out on the course and playing two balls against each other or keeping an aggregate score for the two balls is another example of creative practice. It allows the player to experience different challenges that causes the mind to react and learn instead of relying on rote drills. The drills that are presented here are not for building rote learning but are designed to feel different and stimulate the mind to learn the correct way to hit a shot from a new approach.

Good practice is characterized by incremental learning. You build and refine your skills on a regular basis so that you continue to grow as a player. Attention to the fundamentals is the groundwork for real growth. Once you have learned the basics through practice, you can take them to the course. It would be very unusual to make dramatic improvement in golf just by playing on the course. On the course you are focused on scoring and cannot give the fundamentals and drills for learning time or attention. You can learn etiquette, patience, appreciation of the beauty of golf, and strategy development while playing, but actual shot making and ball striking are developed on the practice range.

When most players hit a poor shot in practice, they shrug it off, drag another ball over, and set it up on a good lie. On the course you have to play that bad shot, so the pressure to concentrate and focus is there. Pressure to perform is what helps us to motivate ourselves to do well. We have to guard against becoming complacent in practice because raking another ball over after a bad shot is just not what we do on a golf course. The practice plan that is laid out above as an example to learn wedge play forces you to take practice seriously enough so that each shot means something. You are not reading a mindless paragraph out of a textbook as in the school example but testing and immersing yourself in the intricacies of wedge play in order to gain insight and understanding of how good shots are produced. You are eliminating complacency or sloppiness, which can lead to indifference and a lack of learning.

When I practice chipping and putting, sometimes I use just one ball and I play the chip shot as if I were on the course. I hit the chip shot and then walk up and size up the putt that I have left as if I were in a tournament. This forces my mind to react as if I were actually in a tournament and had to make the up-and-down. I doubt if I could maintain this level of focus and learning under pressure if I just piled up a pile of balls and chipped one after another until the pile was gone. By practicing in game conditions, you help build the confidence and remove any fear as your skills increase. This approach is based on sound psychological principles.

Many people suffer from phobias—fear of flying in a plane, going on an elevator, or even leaving the house—that restrict their lifestyles to the point that they may not function well in life. Phobias are much more common than most laypeople realize; millions of people of all ages are affected. The major therapy used to help people overcome these fears is called desensitization. To treat fear of flying, the therapist and patient talk about what happens at an airport and what a take-off, flight, and landing involve. The patient and therapist make a trip to an airport, where the patient might visit a ticket counter and watch some planes take off. The next visit may involve walking onto a plane and sitting in a seat. Gradually the fears are diminished until the patient takes an actual flight. In golf, simulating real conditions and feeling the pressure to play well is actually a form of desensitization. The more you practice as you play, the more confident you become, to the point that when the real situation occurs in a tournament the fear and doubt are diminished while confidence to pull the shot off is heightened.

Practice Games and Drills

Games and drills offer the stimulation to learn the golf game more rapidly and with the same type of enjoyment that you get while on the course. Here are some of my favorites.

Accuracy Competition

Select a target down the range, such as a tree. With a player of similar skills, play shot-to-the-target for a dime. Closest to the target wins. In this competition you will want to make sure you are aligned correctly, have picked out an interim target, and then made a swing that emphasizes good fundamentals. The competition makes you concentrate as you would on the course and gets you away from just thoughtlessly machine-gunning balls down range.

Call the Shot

Your competitor calls the type of shot you must hit, for example: hit a low shot; hit a high shot; hit a fade; hit a draw; hit a sharp cut; hit a sharp hook; run a ball along the ground; flop a shot to a near target. You keep hitting the shots until you miss one and then your competitor steps up and you call the shot. All these shots will come into play on the course at one time or another and what better way to learn them than in a friendly competition that simulates real play.

Dialing a Distance

Using one club such as a five-iron, try to hit different distances from 50 yards up to your maximum, which may be about 175 yards for the good player. This game helps you acquire feel. You get to sense what the loft and the amount of force to a swing can do. Your mind absorbs this knowledge in a form that you can call on when on the course. On a windy day you might want to hit a choked-down five-iron to keep the ball out of the wind instead of a full seven-iron for a shot of 150 yards. From your practice, you already have this shot in your bag ready to pull out and use to help you score.

Feet Together

Learning to swing in balance is something you cannot pick up from reading or watching a video. Balance is one of those elements that you develop from doing. A good golf swing must always be in balance so that there is no swaying back and forth. To learn balance, try placing your feet together and hit seven-iron shots with as much of a full swing as you can manage. You will find that you are making a good shoulder turn and that your weight shift actually takes place in miniature as it shifts from the front or back on the backswing and to the front on the downswing. Keep hitting balls this way until you are hitting shots that have good carry and fly accurately. You should not fall off your stance in any way while hitting. When you return to a normal stance you will feel a sense of balance that you never deemed possible.

Learn to Extend

Good extension after impact means that your club head is square and heads down the target line instead of in or out, which is the sign of a poor swing path. Place a tee in the ground about one foot in front of your ball. Hit your drive so that the ball passes over the tee and your driver nicks the tee as it follows the ball. If you are able to nick the tee, you have good extension and you are not swinging from outside in or from inside out.

Learn to Release

Releasing the club means to let the club open and close naturally as your hands and arms move through impact. A good release is essential for power. To exaggerate the feeling of a release hit some balls with your hands held about two inches apart. You will feel how your hands and arms actually work during the swing and will gain an appreciation for what releasing the club means.

Eyes Closed

This is a drill that should help you control your distance so that you are not hitting the ball too far or too short on approaches. Take a sand wedge and line up a shot to your target. Just before starting the club back, close your eyes and complete the swing. Check to see how well you struck the ball and how close you got it to the target. Closing your eyes helps develop your inner eye for visualization; it gives you much better feel for the club as you swing it and it builds your sense of distance.

Impact Drill

This is a drill to help you develop the proper feel of driving through the impact position for solid shots. Take your normal address with a seven-iron. Without moving anything except your wrists, swing the club back so the shaft is parallel to the ground and your hands are still opposite the ball. Now, push off your right foot and make your normal move through impact. The ball will travel only about 30 yards, but the impact should be solid.

Machine-Gun Drill

This drill will help to train your mind to hit good golf shots by letting go and just trying to feel the swing instead of manipulating it. Tee up five balls in a row. Using a five-iron, set up to the first ball and make a normal swing. Without stopping, swing back as you step up to the next ball and hit it and continue until you have hit all five balls. You should have a feeling of freedom and trust after this drill.

Play Your Nemesis

If there is one hole that you fear the most or that always ruins your round, get on top of it in practice by "playing" it over and over. Visualize the hole and actually set up from the tee with the club that you would want to hit for this shot. Note where the ball lands and then visualize the lie and angle to the green or second shot. Play the shot with the club you would most likely hit. Keep score of how well you do. If you hit one into a water hazard, for example, take a penalty and a drop. Play the hole over and over and watch how your scores gradually improve. And the real bonus will be when you go to the course itself and play the hole with no fear. Suddenly the hole will no longer be your nemesis but one that you have conquered hundreds of times in practice.

Using "Swing Thoughts"

Another secret to productive practice is to use "swing thoughts," or mental cues, to develop the skills you want. Swing thoughts should be simple, and you should use only one at a time. Here are some swing thoughts to use as the basis of a practice session:

- "Get to that perfect finish position."
- "Extend the club down the target line."
- "Left shoulder under (my chin), right shoulder under."
- "A one and a two" (for tempo of backswing and downswing).
- "Low and slow" (take-away for your driver).
- "Down and through" (for iron shots, to make sure you take a divot).
- "Light hand and arms."
- "Drive through impact."
- "Get left shoulder behind the ball."

One swing thought should carry you through about a one-hour practice session. Try to maintain focus on what you are trying to accomplish with that session. The shots may not start off very well, but do not get discouraged; if you make the move well in conjunction with your swing thought you will learn and the results will follow. The best part of practicing with one swing thought is that it forces you to concentrate and focus. You are not just beating balls down-range but have a purpose and this purposeful practice accelerates your learning. If you do this two or three times per week and stick to one thought, you are displaying the motivation and discipline to get better and actually demonstrate to yourself that you want to be the best player you can be. This attitude will transcend into your game on the course and into your life as well.

Ask the professional who is giving you lessons and acting as your coach to give you some swing thoughts or cues that are especially tailored to your practice needs. They need to be simple, but not mechanical. They are verbal prompts that trigger your mind to perform an action. Avoid any swing thoughts that are mechanical in nature. Keep it simple so that your mind can easily relate to your move. Studies have shown that the mind can only effectively execute one thought with one movement at a time. "Multitasking" actually refers to a sequence of events; when you do several jobs at work "at the same time," in fact each one is done separately in your mind. Playing the piano incorporates mind with body coordination and results from practice and the development of feel. The piano player could not possible think of each note and where each finger was going to hit that note or there would be no music. Your goal in golf is to become like an accomplished piano player in that your moves become built into your mind so that there is no conscious thought of what your body must do at a certain time. Make music with your swing through practice and feel.

More Tips for Course Practice

Earlier, I mentioned practicing on the course and keeping a two-ball aggregate score as a way of learning. There are other great ways to practice on the course that will make you a better player in a relatively short time. Here are some of my favorites that you can try when your course is empty or not busy.

Go to that one hole that strikes fear into you from the tee. Hit shots from this tee using a driver, three-wood, or fairway wood and evaluate which club gets you into your desired position most often. This is your tee shot for that hole when you play for real. Keep hitting that tee shot until you feel totally confident that you can place a good shot off of the tee every time.

Go looking for trouble. If you are playing a round by yourself, take a look at trouble spots on each hole. Place your ball in a trouble spot and practice how to get out of it. Hit balls under and over trees, out of the deepest bunker, or from heavy rough near the green and make that downhill chip onto a fast green. When these shots come up in a round, you will already know what to expect. Only the very best players practice like this—maybe that partly explains why they are the very best. Think of how many times you got into one of the above situations and came away from the hole with a 7 or 8 on your scorecard. The good player expects to have some trouble shots and learns in advance how to handle them. Later on, we will discuss strategy and how to hit trouble shots.

Keep a book for your course. All touring pros make out a course book while they play a practice round. On each hole they note which clubs they hit from a particular spot. They note where there are undulations in the fairway and greens and how the ball reacts as it lands on the fairway or green. You should do the same. Make notes as to what club you should hit from a particular spot. Learn to evaluate the places on the hole that will allow you the easiest access to the green. Make notes on each hole as you play your course and you will develop good learning habits on how to improve. Keep the book in your bag and pull it out on the tee for a little refresher course before you play the hole.

Every course has subtle features that you will only learn to deal with through experience. For example, on my course there is one green that is soft on one side and hard on the other, as a result of how the water drains from a nearby slope. If you hit to a pin on the left side of this green, the ball will hit and stick or spin back. If you hit to a pin on the right side, you have to make sure you land it short, as the ball will bounce and roll. If you were new to the course or had just played it five or ten times, you might never realize what was going on with the shots that you were hitting into this green unless somebody told you or you finally discovered it yourself. (We will discuss course strategy in more detail in chapter 4.)

Pre- and Post-round Practice Routine

Pre- and post-round practice have specific roles to play as you develop your golf game.

Pre-round Practice

The goals of a pre-round practice routine are to warm up and stretch your muscles for play, wake up your eye-hand coordination skills, build confidence for your round, test playing conditions, and note how your body and golf swing are relating. The day before a tournament or important round, I go through the following routine:

- The night before, I eat a nutritional and easy-to-digest meal. Usually I prefer seafood and a salad and I avoid coffee. Avoid alcohol, spicy foods, or sleeping aids, as they will have an adverse effect on you in the morning. We all have sleep rhythms that should remain constant if we are to feel well, so I go to bed at my normal time. Too little or too much sleep will throw you off for the next day.
- I wake up early. Studies of students taking standardized tests have shown that student who woke up earlier did better than those who slept closer to the test time. The reason the researchers gave for this was that the brain needs time to fully wake up and function at full capacity after a period of sleep. Eat a light but satisfying breakfast. Avoid sweets such as doughnuts, as they tend to give you a quick sugar rush followed by a slow down as your body processes the sugar. One coffee is the limit, as caffeine can cause the jitters in some people, and this will not help you putt those three-footers very well.
- I watch a video of Tom Purtzer's swing before I play, as his great move helps to sink into my mind and stay with me once I start to swing. Watching a video of a great swing over and over for about five minutes helps you to gain a visual sense of rhythm and tempo for the day.
- I like to go for a short walk and breathe the morning air and relax my mind. This is not a power walk. The walk simply gets my muscles warmed and also loosens my lower-back muscles.
- I go through a series of stretches, which I show you in chapter 6. Stretching allows my muscles to become flexible and gives me a feeling of being loose and supple. Sam Snead referred to having a feeling of being "oily" throughout his body.
- Then I meditate for about five minutes. This is probably the most important part of my pre-round routine. I use a system of progressive muscle relaxation that was developed by Dr. Herbert Benson

of Harvard University and described in his book *The Relaxation Response*. I follow the muscle relaxation with another period of meditation in which my mind becomes free and relaxed. At the end of this period, I feel energized and alert and ready to play golf.

Relaxing and Meditating

Here is my adaptation of the relaxation response and my meditation technique with visualization:

Sit in a comfortable chair or lie on your bed. Place your hands together and squeeze them hard while you count to five, then gradually release the pressure as you count back from five to one.

Lift your shoulders straight up to your ears and hold them raised as you count from one to five and then, as you release, from five to one. As you release this time feel your arms lie still at your side and imagine warm water washing all the tension from your shoulders, down your arms, and out your fingers. Lie or sit still with nothing but the thought of the water washing away the tension.

Repeat the tensing-and-release pattern in your abdomen, legs, and finally your face. Repeat the visualization of water cleansing and relaxing these muscle groups.

When you finish with your face, feel the water smooth your forehead and make your jaw go slack. You should feel totally relaxed and your mind will have a feeling of being light but calm. Scientists have established that this type of relaxation routine increases the level of theta waves in our brains; these waves calm us, reduce stress, and actually lower blood pressure. Relaxation and meditation simultaneously decreases the level of alpha waves, which are the stimulation that our brains receive and react to.

These exercises quiet and focus your mind. They allow you to focus by filtering out the "noise" that assaults our minds while they relax us to a point where stress cannot cause tension to influence our bodies or affect our thinking.

The next step involves breathing so that your stomach goes out slowly as you inhale and comes in slowly when you exhale. This is the kind of breathing that you will take to the course with you. As you breathe in you take in energy and positive feelings and as you exhale you release tension and all negative feeling so that you build a feeling of well-being.

Visualization

Finally, I visualize the most beautiful place on earth. Maybe a waterfall surrounded by flowers and jungle, or a sandy beach with clear water and a blue sky and drifting birds. I feel a soft breeze on my face and enjoy the enrichment that this natural beauty brings me. This is a special place that you can visit anytime once you learn to relax and let your mind take you there. In effect, once your visualization skills are finely tuned, your mind will barely register whether you are visualizing the natural beauty or are actually there.

I remain at this beautiful place and enjoy it for several minutes. I gradually count from ten to one and with the word "one" I awaken from my meditation state and feel ready for the day.

Please do not be skeptical about the mental powers that you can harness and the benefits of this type of relaxation and visualization. The mind is your most powerful ally in accomplishing what you want to do with your life and your time. If you exercise and tune your mind so that it functions at its highest level, you will reap the benefits.

If you find it difficult to meditate on your own, there are relaxation tapes that can induce meditation or you can find fitness facilities and spas that offer training in meditation, stretching, and relaxation. Music to help you meditate is readily available in every music store. This whole process of meditation may only take five to ten minutes but you will start your day in a way that lets you enjoy the rest of your waking hours. This is another tool that will move you up the ladder of success in golf. It will separate you from the average player, who never travels to such places and has not learned to work with a mind that is tension-free and ready to respond for us and not work against us.

Dress for Success

I like to dress for success. I put my clothes out the night before and make sure that everything looks well together (I have my wife sign off on it) and that everything is pressed and neat. My shoes are cleaned or polished and ready to go. If you dress well, you tend to perform better, as you show that you genuinely care about your presentation and express your sense of self-worth and self-esteem. When I worked as a psychologist, I could dress in any way I wanted, but I always chose to dress professionally, in a suit or jacket and tie. I always felt that my clients would sense my commitment to professionalism from my attention to my presentation and it served to subtly remind me to always do my best as a professional. When you see someone playing in jeans and a T-shirt on a course, you feel that he or she is not a true golfer or does not have a genuine ambition to become a good golfer. I once asked the vice president of the PGA Tour why touring professionals could not wear shorts on hot days. He replied that they were professionals and they want to present the same look as you would expect from professionals in a business setting.

Tee Timing

I like to arrive about an hour and a half before my tee time. Sometimes there are administrative things to take care of such as registration and finding your way around that might set you off your time. The last thing you want is to have to jump out of your car and run to the first tee.

I head for the practice range with the goals of developing solid contact, building my confidence, and seeing how the ball is reacting on this day.

I start with a sand wedge. The sand wedge is the heaviest club in your bag, so this is the club that will help build your swing path for the day. Starting by hitting solid shots with the sand wedge is not just a golfer's superstition; it is a great principle for setting your muscles up to swing properly for your round. I make a short backswing and accelerate into the ball, hitting down and through. My main thought here is to hit the ball in the center of the club face and make solid contact with every shot. I try to concentrate very hard on making these first swings all be solid shots, as they tend to set me up for hitting solid shots with all my clubs for the rest of the day. I gradually increase the length of the backswing and distance of the shots that I hit with the sand wedge. I cannot overemphasize the importance of this portion of the practice, as solid shots seem to flow from this early stage of warm-up.

Next I gradually start working through the bag, hitting the pitching wedge, then moving up to a nine-iron, and on up to the longer clubs. The goal is to feel the clubs and make solid contact.

You might find that your ball has a slight fade or a slight draw on this particular day. Don't try to change it; just make up your mind that you will play with it for this day. Our bodies change, and these little things can happen for no apparent reason. Just accept them and adapt to them for the day.

Hit some fairway woods from the ground and from a tee to get the feel of the two ways that you may use them on the course.

Round out your full swings with some driver practice. Use a smooth swing and concentrate on solid contact that puts your ball in the fairway. Do not try to put on a long driving demonstration or tire yourself out. Finish when you are hitting your driver down the middle and feel in control of your swing.

The final phase is a testing phase. Find some rough that resembles the rough on the course and hit a few wedge shots to see how the ball comes out and how it affects the club head. Find a practice bunker and hit a few shots to test the texture of the green. Finally, go to the practice green to learn the speed of the green and the effect that the grain has on the ball. Hit some long putts to see how the ball travels over the green—whether it is fast or slow, smooth or choppy. Hit some 30-foot putts and try to stop them up against the fringe. This will help you get a feel in your mind for the speed that you can use on the greens on the course. Finally, hit some three-foot putts so that they all go into the hole. Listen to the ball drop into the cup over and over as this will build your confidence. Avoid attempting putts that you most likely will miss, as this will only have you practicing failing. Remember, your goal at this stage is building confidence, not learning a putting stroke.

Walk to the first tee with your head up and expectations high. Feel confident that you are well prepared and that you can trust your swing to do what you need it to do for the day. Smile to yourself in anticipation of playing well and having an enjoyable day. Let those neuro-transmitters send positive waves flowing through your mind and fill you with self-esteem. Tee your ball up and make the best swing possible.

Post-round Practice Routine

Post-round practice is not for everyone. If you are tired or mentally drained it is better to forgo this extra practice. You must guard against injuries and you will not gain anything from practicing while you are tired. But if you are young and working to get to a very high level of play, then this type of practice should be part of your routine.

You may have two reasons to go to the range for a post-round session: either you hit the ball so great that you want to hit more shots to keep the feeling going and help your body and mind remember what great shots feel like, or you had a fault, such as blocked drives or wedge shots that flew too high. In this case you will work just on that fault and try to correct it so that it does not creep into your mind at night or remain there the next day. But if you had a day when you just could not hit the ball well at all, forget the post-round play, as you do not want to practice when you are out of sync with yourself. Just put the clubs away and erase the bad day from your mind.

The Practice Journal

It is a good idea to keep a practice journal as part of your overall approach to improvement. In your journal, record the date, length of practice, what you were working on, and what kind of results you obtained. It is a great idea to write down some swing thought or particular correction that you made that helped you. We tend to forget changes and drift back to what is comfortable. By keeping a journal, you become a researcher who continually tracks change, progress, and results.

It may also be useful to read your journal in the morning or the night before playing a round to review what aspects of your game are changing and what swing thoughts or changes to bring to the course. So many players say that they hit the ball great at the range but can't seem to replicate it on the course. The journal is one way to bridge that gap.

Mental Disciplines

Practice is meant to build both physical and mental skills.

Feedback

Feedback is very important on the practice range as it is your mind's report to you on how you are doing. When you hit a good shot you should pause and place that memory, flight of the ball, and feeling in the hands all into your mind. You might add something to help you recall and bring that sensory feedback to yourself on the course or anytime that you need a surge of confidence. One tool used in therapy is to have a client use an "anchor" to stimulate a thought or feeling that will help him or her feel a particular way or remember a sensation that helps cope with a situation. An anchor to remember a wonderful drive might be to touch the side of your cheek after hitting a drive in practice that is long and straight. On the course, all you have to do is touch your cheek, and the visualization of your swing and the ball flight will come back to you and instill confidence. I read of a touring professional who had first-tee jitters with large crowds during his first year out. A sports psychologist had him pull the bill of his cap lower over his eyes on the first tee. In practice he went through a little drill of pulling the bill down lower and stepping up to a ball as if it were the first tee. This anchor caused him to block out his awareness of the crowd. The fear left him and his only thought was hitting a great drive.

Control Negative Emotions

When you hit a bad shot in practice, do not become upset. It did not cost you a stroke and everyone hits them in practice. This is actually a learning opportunity for your play on the course. Learn to accept the shot and understand why it happened. Dismiss it as part of your game and simply accept it as a mistake that you made but now know how to correct.

Anger does not help us at all in golf. It may in football or hockey, where adrenaline must increase to enhance performance, but the opposite is true in golf. Practice sessions offer us little rehearsal times for us to deal with frustration and anger and remove them to get back to playing well. If a player on the range is slamming his club or cursing out loud, not a lot of learning about the golf swing is going on, and even less about emotional control.

Memory

Use your power of recall to analyze and correct mistakes. Try to replay the bad shot in your mind and feel or even visualize the swing that caused the bad shot. Compare it with a previous swing that hit the ball perfectly and see if you can discern the differences. Hours of practice and experience give good players the ability to know what went wrong almost immediately. In a recent tournament, Tiger Woods was trying to hit a high fade with a long iron into a green. The shot flew right and short of the target, and Tiger said to his caddy immediately, "I wiped it," meaning that he had cut across the ball without striking it solidly. As you become a better golfer, your ability to know what went wrong will grow.

Passion

The player who wants to become good—or great—must practice with intensity. To get where you want, you have to be willing to commit to it. This does not mean grinding every shot in practice. But you should sense your swing and know when your mind and body are firing together with each swing to produce the results that you want. You must increase both quality and quantity of practice in order to become a better player. There is no gimmick or quick fix that can suddenly turn you into a Tour-level player, even though some videos and swing aids make such promises. Lee Trevino once said, "Anyone can become a Tour player; all you have to do is hit a million balls." You may never have the time, opportunity, or will to practice at that level of intensity, but increased practice is the only way to improve. Players who have the same handicaps that they had ten years ago probably hit a bucket or two of balls at the range with no real plan. The good and great players develop their games in all aspects in a planned and serious manner with a specific goal in mind.

Work Ethic

Having played on minitours and practiced at facilities such as Doral, in Miami, where touring professionals train, I am familiar with their work ethic. You may not want to make your living at the game, but you can learn about what it takes to get to the next level. If you dream of becoming a single-digit player or a club champion, or even turning professional, practice is your vehicle to reach your goal. Practice mindfully, so that every swing is made with the intent of sensing the correct tempo and rhythm that will become your natural swing at all times.

Gradually increase your practice time. Remember that you are not beating balls but developing specific skills that will become part of your makeup through thought and feel. Remain fit, hydrated, and rested while practicing, and increase the length of time and number of shots that you hit with each session. Great players spend days on the range and their practice comes back to them as great play on the course and in tournaments. I have seen touring professionals hit balls on a range for hours and hours with or without a coach. This quality and quantity of practice separates the average golfer from the good and great ones. If you choose to become the latter, you must make the commitment to do what has to be done to make it.

Attitude

When I was a youngster, there were times when I practiced so long that my hands would bleed in places from hitting so many shots. My mother was upset at my practicing to the point of pain, but she could not understand my love of and drive to be good at this game. I was very young and free to be totally consumed by practice. But adults need to be more sensible. Please do not practice to the point of fatigue or risk injury in any way. You must follow sound advice on taking care of your body and mind while developing your game and guard against excess.

Somebody will yell, "Keep your head down" and that will be it. Be like a child when it comes to learning, though. Every shot, every hole, and every swing is a learning opportunity for you. Every time you hit a good shot, it is something to store and draw on when you play the shot again. Every poor shot is a means of testing your knowledge and feel to analyze how to correct it and to design steps to solve the problem. Poor golfers hit bad shots and have no idea why it happened. Good golfers also hit bad shots, but they learn from them.

If you start to hit a series of bad shots such as shanks or topped shots, you have slipped into a temporary funk that you need to get away from instantly. When this happens, I put the club down and go get a soda or take a little walk on the range or just sit on a bench for a while. I do my breathing and relaxation routine to calm and refresh my mind. I then return to the practice session, get back into my routine, and start over. This little mental vacation and refresher will cure the funk and when you return to practice, your good swing will be back.

Remember that practice is fun, not work. It is an enjoyable time, filled with discovery and challenges that cannot be matched by any other experience when you use creativity and function in a learning mode. Many times, I prefer to practice rather than play as I get to hit more golf shots and I get to experiment. I feel a greater sense of accomplishment from getting better than just posting a good score.

To keep fresh on the practice range, take breaks on a regular basis between clubs or sequences in your practice plan. I like to walk along the range and find a golfer who has a great swing and watch him or her hit balls. Try not to watch players who have a poor, awkward, or quick swing, as these characteristics can slip into your mind as well. When I am on the course, if I am playing with a player who has an awkward move I look down toward the target so as to avoid having the vision of a poor swing in my mind. I also never watch left-handers swing as it offers a contrarian view of the golf swing. The left-hander may have a great swing with good tempo but it may confuse your inner eye. Maybe left-handers should not watch right-handers swing. Or this may be my own superstition. Superstition and strange idiosyncrasies are part of the golfer's makeup—it's just another thing that makes golf special.

Faults and Fixes

The practice range is the place to fix what is wrong with your game. Earlier, we discussed going to a professional and getting proper instruction to learn the swing and the fundamentals. After the lesson practice the skills that you learned. When you have flaws that cause problems on the course it is always a good idea to see a pro to help find a cure. As a life-long learner, however, you should be able to go to the practice range and work out many of your problem shots through knowledge and experience rather than having a lesson every time something goes wrong. The key is to recognize the problem and examine possible causes. In practice, you can correct most of the common flaws by running through a little checklist as a mechanic would in diagnosing and fixing a problem with your car. Let's take a look at some common problems and the cures that you can use to stay on track to good golf.

Remember, the two things that control the flight and direction of a golf ball are the angle of the club face at impact and path of the club head through impact. It sounds simple, but that's all the physics there is to how a ball is hit on a straight line. If a ball flies off at an unwanted angle or curves in the air the cause has to be in one of the two factors listed above. A ball that does not get airborne or flies farther than wanted occurs when the club face comes into the ball at the wrong height. Too low and we hit the ground behind it and the ball is pushed by the turf; too high and the ball is hit in the equator or on top and is sent off in a low-line drive or a ground ball. The lie of the ball can also affect the flight path.

The Slice

Almost every beginning golfer starts off slicing the ball from right to left. It seems very natural to swing so that club comes from the outside of the target line and strikes the ball in a way that produces a spin that curves the ball from left to right. The average golfer tends to give up on trying to fix the slice and learns to live with it. More than just living with it, the average golfer will set up in a way that will ensure that he or she continues to hit the slice. This is homeostasis in action: not changing the status quo because change is too hard and disruptive.

Actually, the slice is quite curable. Most players set up incorrectly, so that they have an open stance with their front foot pulled back from the target line. The hips, shoulders, and feet all point to the right—also incorrect. The golfer will swing on a plane that brings the club head from the outside and across the ball so that it spins in a way to cause the slice left to right. A simple way to cure this would be to reverse the setup to a closed position and let the player experience a feeling of hitting the ball by swinging inside to out, which tends to cause a hook or a draw. I have had students who were not willing even to try this change, as it seems opposed to everything that they have learned. They feel that if they aim to the right, the ball will fly right and slice even more to the right.

There is an easier and more visual way to cure a poor swing path. Place a length of two-by-four parallel to the target line with the ball, a few inches away from the ball. The golfer will not be able to hit the ball with an outside-to-inside swing path as the board will stop the club. If you are afraid of hitting a board while learning a good swing path, place a head cover or towel outside the ball instead. Set up square so that your body lines up straight and parallel to your target line. Hit the balls so that you do not touch the board or head cover with your club. Suddenly you will see the ball flying straight or maybe a left to right draw. This is the correction for the swing path.

A club face that is open at impact will also cause a slice. Correcting this usually involves correcting your grip, as explained in chapter 2. If you slice, chances are you have your right hand turned too far to your left—on top of the shaft—in what is a called a weak grip. The result is that your hands will not release enough to close the club face through impact. Place your hands so that your thumbs lie on the sides of the shaft, as explained earlier, grip the club lightly, and try not to get in your own way by manipulating your hands through impact. If you are reading this book, chances are that you have passed your slicing stage, but you should still have the basic knowledge of how to make the correction in case you find yourself falling into a case of the slices.

Fat Shots

"Fat shots" occur when your club strikes the turf behind the ball. A real fat shot is when you "lay turf" over the ball! Most good players will not do that, but may hit the turf slightly behind the ball so that the flight of the ball is shortened and the strike is not crisp. The most common cause of this slight error is getting a little too quick as you start your downswing. The hands and arms start down in a way that races ahead of the weight shift or your move into the ball and sets the low point of your swing just behind the ball at impact. On the practice range, make sure that your hands are slightly forward at address, and, most important, start down from the top smoothly. The move down starts with the lower body; the arms and hands should begin slowly and build speed as they near impact. When you practice, use the "A one and a two" swing thought, which ensures that you start down slowly.

The Blocked Shot

Probably the most common of all faults among good players is the blocked shot, one that strikes the ball well but sends it to the right of the target. Even touring professionals hit this shot from time to time and with some, it creeps into their games in spurts. The blocked shot is so called because the swing is blocked by your body. The golfer must turn his or her hips out of the way to allow the arms and hands to pass through the impact zone on a square path. If the lower body does not clear out, the arms are forced to hit from a very inside-to-outside path.

The Wild Shot

The cause of a drive or shot that flies well to the right is the opposite of the blocked shot and occurs with good players, when their bodies race ahead of their arms and hands. Sometimes when players want to hit a long drive, they correctly try to speed up the hip and shoulder turn to generate more club-head speed. The problem occurs when the club lags too far behind the body or gets "stuck" behind while the body moves ahead. When the arms and hands try to play catch-up at impact, the club face has not had enough time to get square.

If you seem to be hitting one or two wild drives per round when you try to crank one up, you may be getting the club stuck behind you. In practice, try to get your hands a little higher over your left shoulder at the top of the swing to build a longer arc rather than trying to gain extra distance by speeding up your body or, worse, your arms and hands. Changing your tempo to hit a ball longer or shorter is never a good idea for players at any level. You can get wider and longer with your arc and keep your tempo and produce longer shots. To gear back on a shot, choke down on the handle and still keep the same tempo. Speed kills.

The Pulled Shot

Every good player will pull a shot from time to time. This is a well-struck shot that flies well left of the target. The pulled shot usually is the result of not making a good weight shift from your back to your front foot before starting down. If you hang back on your right foot, chances are you will spin your upper body and hit it well left. You will get a feeling of swaying forward into the ball instead of setting the left side and firing through with the right.

The following drill will help you make a good weight shift and rid yourself of pulled shots. Use a five-iron and stand with your feet together and the ball about six inches in front of your left foot and on your target line. Swing back with your feet still together and then step forward as you reach the top of your swing. Do not stop but simply let the shift of your weight help start the club down toward impact. You will feel that the weight shifting onto the front foot pulls the club into the hitting zone as your head stays in place. The feeling of swaying occurs when your body tries to get to the left side without making the proper shift with the lower body. This drill will force you to get the feel of working the lower body properly.

The Hook

Occasionally, a hook—when the ball flies in a big curve to the left—may cause you to hit a ball out of bounds or lose it. A single-digit player will have the fundamentals of grip, stance, and posture in place, so those should be eliminated as the culprits. When a pro or good player hits a hook it is usually caused by letting go from the top or coming over the ball with the right shoulder.

Letting go with the hands or casting the club as a fisherman casts a net lets the club head get out in front of your hands so that the club face is closed at impact and the ball is struck with a hook spin. In practice, you can make sure that you hold your hands in the cocked position by doing a pumping drill. Swing back to the top and start down holding your hands in place as if you were pulling a rope on a bell. Stop your downswing halfway down with your hands still in the cocked position. Go back up to the top and start back down and finish the swing through impact and follow-through. This drill forces you to get the feeling of keeping the hands in the correct position as you start down and prevents your hands from getting ahead at impact.

Often you will hear a TV announcer say that a pro "came over the top" of a shot that was hooked or landed well left of the target. Coming over the top is usually the result of trying to hit the ball too hard from the top of the swing. The right shoulder juts out as the downswing begins so the club head comes into the ball from an outside-to-inside swing path but hits the ball squarely to the left or the hands close a bit and the result is a pulled hook.

My favorite cure for coming over the top (and several other faults as well) is to place a headcover under your right armpit as you hit balls. You must hit the balls without having the headcover fall to the ground. This forces you to stay connected—your shoulder and arms cannot jut away from your body but must stay close to your side and chest as they move through impact. It is a simple cure and very effective. You will be surprised at how well you make contact while doing this. I think that if it were legal under the rules of golf, many players would put a headcover under their arms for every shot.

The Shank

A shank is a ball that is struck on the hosel of the club and flies terribly to the right and short. The shank can be demoralizing, as it usually occurs on a short shot and ends up getting you in deep trouble. Some golfers think shanks are contagious and fear that if they see someone hit a shank, they, too, will start to hit them. Shanks are not contagious, but they can sneak into a good player's swing suddenly. There are two main causes for this dreaded shot: your weight is too much toward your toes as you swing down, or your backswing is pulled to the inside too quickly.

You can correct the weight problem by simply practicing shifting your weight back and forth a little at address and then settling the weight on the insides and the balls of your feet. If you are playing a shot with the ball well below your feet, gravity may pull your weight toward your toes on the downswing and cause a shank. During practice, find a slope such that you can place the ball below your feet. Swing so that your legs are "quiet"—do not move much—and most of your swing is done with the upper body. You should have a feeling of keeping your heels in place as you swing and make a good shoulder turn.

To correct the snatching of the club back to the inside too quickly, place a two-by-four board that extends back from your toe line. As you swing back make sure that the club does not hit or cross over the top of the board. This will prevent you from snatching the club to the inside, then shanking the ball by coming into impact from a severe inside-to-out swing path. Use this drill in practice if shanks sneak into your swing while practicing. On the course, make several practice backswings while ensuring that the club starts straight back along the target line. You might make a slight waggle that goes straight back from the ball prior to the take-away as a little rehearsal to eliminate any possibility of the shank.

Shots That Fly Too Low

Accomplished players may find that somehow, the ball flight has changed and the ball is landing and bouncing on the green too much instead of landing and stopping. Usually this is not caused by ball striking but by a little change that may have crept into your posture. A low ball flight is usually caused by a swing plane that is too flat. Think of a pane of glass placed over the plane that your club travels and imagine it tilted down to create a sharper angle or tilted less, so that it is flatter. A flat swing plane is caused either by too much bending in your knees, so that your back gets upright, or too much bending from your hips, which throws your balance forward. Check your posture in a mirror from behind. See that your arms hang down and slightly out from your shoulders but do not seem to be reaching out to the ball.

It is always a good idea to check your posture or have a pro look at your address position from time to time, as little flaws can develop without our noticing them. We may think we are in a good position because it feels comfortable, whereas in actuality we have fallen into a bad habit and our body has adapted to the subtle change over time.

In summary, practice is the workshop for improvement. You must be willing to give time to practice as this separates the bad from the good and the good from the great. Your time is precious, so use the practice time wisely to develop skills and feel the proper swing. Use your knowledge and advice from your pro to develop sound practice plans. Always have a purpose to your practice so that you have something in mind to develop, enhance or correct every time you step onto the range. Take quality time over quantity when it comes to practicing any aspect of your game. Always take your time between shots to reinforce your fundamentals.

Every shot in practice should be hit with the same care that you would give to a shot on the course. Always select a target and check your grip, alignment, stance, and posture. Work to feel a rhythm and tempo to your swing that repeats consistently every time. This type of practice will allow you to play the game of golf when you are on the course instead of working at it or struggling with it. Think of Deepak Chopra's advice: Do not struggle. Practice does not bind you; it gives you freedom. On the course you can be free of mechanical and analytical left-brain thinking. Through practice you will master the mechanics of hitting a golf ball long and straight. On the course you are free to be creative, evaluate options, visualize shots, and allow your mind to energize and empower you to play well.

When counseling my children, I would often remind them that even though they were in the early stages of school they were not just getting ready for life but were actually living it in the present. As golfers trying to improve, we can get caught up in the future and forget that we are in the present. Although your goal may be to be a single-handicap, scratch, or professional, the practice that you are undertaking is not just a means to that end but a part of your golfing life that should be enjoyed and cherished. If practice becomes drudgery it is no longer fruitful. Your appreciative realm of learning will stop lighting the fire to see the beauty of a ball in flight or one that strikes a target. Learn to love the game a swing at a time. Practice is part of the game.

CHAPTER FOUR

Thinking on the Course

ONE OF THE GREAT ASPECTS OF GOLF THAT SEPARATES IT FROM OTHER sports is the importance that is placed on the mind and not just the body. Mind work in golf goes far beyond selecting what club to hit or reading a putt correctly. Good golfers are in tune with the higher levels and different types of mind activity while they play. The educational psychologist Benjamin Bloom developed a taxonomy of the cognitive domain, a definitive work on skills to be acquired, and in his scheme *metacognition* is the highest form of mental functioning.

Metacognition is the planning, assessing, and monitoring of one's own thinking process. It is the pinnacle of mental functioning because we look upon ourselves as if we were outside looking in on our patterns of thinking. This is not some esoteric, irrelevant notion. For golfers who want to achieve their aspirations, it is essential to be able to evaluate the quality and efficacy of their thoughts and feelings.

In golf, the mental aspect is critical to good play. Figuring out and strategizing one's way around a course is a difficult and complex task that is based on learning, experience, and intuition. Our thinking comes not only from the past experience that we have acquired from our golfing lives, but also from our belief system itself. Emotional well-being is also integral to producing good results on the golf course. How we see ourselves and how we trust ourselves to perform are as important as knowing what to do.

In this chapter we will look at the types of thinking that we do on a golf course, including our emotional responses. The goal is for you to become aware of what types of thinking exist, what influences our thinking and perceptions, and how we react—what results are produced from that brain activity. While you may forget the word "metacognition," you will carry a framework of monitoring and assessing your thinking to see whether you are on track, whether you are confident and clear. In particular, you should be able to see how you make decisions, evaluate options, and understand how emotions play a role in your performance.

Types of Thinking

Numerous ways of thinking have been identified by psychologists and educators. This list is not exhaustive but includes types of thinking that apply readily to playing the game of golf;

- *Inductive thought.* This type of thinking involves making a decision or drawing conclusions from the information that is presented to you. An example of inductive thought in golf is perceiving the strength of the wind and then deciding what type of shot will work best in this wind condition.
- *Deductive thought.* Thinking deductively means asking yourself, "What is going on here, what rules apply, and what will probably happen?" Reading a chip shot from the rough near a green calls on deductive thought as you must figure that the heavy grass will probably come between the club face and ball so the ball will most likely have little back spin and will roll farther than normal.
- *Error analysis.* This form of thinking is about asking whether there is something wrong with our evaluation of a situation that needs to be corrected. An example might be finding that the greens are much slower than they look or there is more break in the putts than you would reasonably expect and figuring out why.
- *Abstracting.* This form of thinking has to do with recognizing relationships. You might conclude that your loss of distance with your driver is caused by a stance you are taking that is too wide or too narrow for your normal swing. You are able to see the whys

of what is going on with your game and find cause-and-effect relationships.

- *Decision making.* You have to decide what to do for a particular shot or situation. We need to be able to make sound decisions on the course. Critical thinking, or what to believe, is part of the decision-making process that we will explore.
- *Problem solving.* The ability to look at an adverse situation and weigh options. In golf, this may involve lying up in front of a water hazard instead of going for the green with a risky shot.
- *Emotional management.* The role of our emotions is vitally important to our performance on the course. Emotions are a type of thought that affects our physical performance and can enhance or hinder our ability to use our thinking skills efficiently.

The types of thinking do not happen in some sequence or occur independently. In fact, you may employ all these types of thinking simultaneously as you apply your mind to a situation during the round. Let's look at a typical example. If you have a ball in an unplayable lie you may use inductive and deductive thought to analyze what has happened and what options are available to you as well as what might happen should you choose each option available. You are solving a problem and making a decision on the basis of the inductive and deductive information you are receiving. You scan your mind to see if there is something faulty with your thinking that got you into this position, to check whether you are making a decision based on some misperception such as "I can just hack that ball out of there instead of taking an unplayable." Finally, you need to assess how this situation has affected your emotional state. Are anger and frustration present? Is tension creeping in? How am I talking to myself?

You are playing a match and you are one up on the 18th hole. You and your opponent have both hit great drives down the middle and have about 220 yards over a pond in front of the green on this par-5. You are away. You have the ability to reach the green in two if you hit a good three-wood. There is some trouble over the green if you go too far, and of course there is the water hazard covering the entire area in front of the green. Your opponent is a good player and is also capable of reaching the green in two if he hits his fairway wood well.

If you land on the green, you will have two putts to make birdie and will win the match, as your opponent would have to make an eagle just to halve the match and send it to extra hole. That would be improbable from the distance that he has to hit his shot. If you land in the water, you will have to take a drop and you will be hitting your fourth shot from about 100 yards, again over water. You would need one putt to make a par, which would mean that you would probably have to hit your fourth shot close. If you make a bogey, you will probably lose the hole.

Another option is to lay up with a five-iron that would put you in the fairway and leave you with a nine-iron to the green and then two putts to make a par, which means your opponent must make a birdie to send the match to extra holes. You think of how you have played this hole in the past and how well you hit your three-wood and how well you can hit your five-iron. You reach into your bag.

The situation above brings into play many facets of thinking on the golf course. It would be interesting and it would tell a great deal about you if you analyzed the situation above carefully and then gave your honest answer as to what you would do. Your emotional state will have a lot to do with your decision making. We presented some inductive and deductive thinking above to analyze what the situation had in store for us and we used analytical thinking to draw relationships between our choices and possible results. Is your emotional state one of total confidence in hitting a three-wood onto the green to defiantly put the *coup de grace* on your opponent? Does your error analysis look upon this thinking as not being in your best interest as you should lay up, make a sure par, and force your opponent to make birdie?

The situation above is just an example of how in a very short time we must take in information, process it, delve into our minds to discern past experiences, and assess our capabilities and then check on our emotional component to see if it fits with our rational side. Our minds are intricate and truly wondrous in the abilities we possess to assimilate, process, and execute in a short time frame and under pressure. Despite the technological advances in microprocessors and computer operating systems, scientists tell us that it would take a computer the size of a city block to do what the human brain is capable of doing. I point this out only to emphasize that your mind is a your best piece of golfing equipment.

When I look at Tiger Woods or Annika Sorenstam, I see athletes who were blessed with physical abilities for sure but also players who have superior thinking skills. They were able to learn the game and adapt, refine, and hone their swings and shot-making skills through practice and careful thought. They know how to manage their games and their emotional states on the course. They know themselves very well, have high self-esteem, and are perfectly confident in their ability to do well. They have set goals for themselves and planned how to achieve them. Everything they do on the golf course and practice range is done with precise thought and higher thinking skills. They stand tall in their field for the same reason others rise to the top in other areas. They think in the realm of metacognition. They are aware of what is going on within their minds and bodies and use that skill to produce incredible results.

We may never approach the abilities that those golfers have but we can strive to emulate the thinking skills that have propelled them to the top. We will look at how to strategize and adjust on the course, to take in information and process it, to develop concentration and relaxation, and to function in a productive emotional state. You already have the tools to do these things right now. Thinking like a champion golfer is one way of making dramatic improvement as a player. Everything you need is inside you. You need only to recognize and exercise those aspects of your thinking to develop them in a way that allows you to excel.

Thinking Your Way Around the Course

Course management or course strategy deals with how you think and manage yourself as you play a course. Since management skills have nothing to do with physical ability, you can improve your game simply by being a better thinker, decision maker, and analyzer on the course. You do not need to be a great player to be a great course manager but you do need to be a great course manager to be a great player. In order to take your game to the next level, you must learn how to get around the course in the fewest strokes. Practice and actual play that places awareness on thinking actually will help you rewire your brain. Your mind will learn new ways to approach a shot; it will develop links on thoughts and how to execute them and will build a resource base for your decision making.

All players hit some bad shots in every round. Ben Hogan said that he only expected to hit two or three really good shots per round. The winner in golf is actually the player who makes the fewest mistakes and who misses closer to the target. I do not get too upset with myself if I hit a poor shot while playing. Sure, it's temporarily unnerving, but recovering and going on to score well is part of the game. What I truly get upset with myself about is making a mental mistake while playing. Mental mistakes are the result of not concentrating or not going through the thought process outlined after our example. Sometimes, I feel, mental errors creep in when players become tired, sloppy, or nervous. The best thing to do to develop your conscious thought process is to be aware that you must go through one on each shot and also become aware of your emotional state, which may be influencing your thinking.

By becoming aware that you must focus and concentrate on the task at hand—the shot in front of you—you activate your mind to sense and detect data and then process the information in an analytical way. This may seem rather obvious to you, but it is far from evident to most golfers.

As a Marine, I went through three weeks of desert training once in the Mojave Desert. The temperatures were well into the 100s every day and the heat was relentless. We were schooled in water discipline, move-ment and safety, and equipment function in hot conditions, but no one mentioned the ability to think to us prior to our training exercise. Within the first few days we began to notice that some simple tasks such as doing math calculations for logistics suddenly became diffi-cult. It seemed as if all at once we noticed that our brain functioning had slowed down much as our bodies did in the heat. It was just our natural homeostatic response to slow down to conserve energy and fluids in our bodies.

The desert training taught me how environment can affect thinking in remarkable ways. It taught me to keep my body fueled and in shape to guard against becoming tired and sloppy with my thinking. Most of all it gave me an awareness that when it comes to thinking we do not always function at our peak, for many reasons. We can lose focus because of our emotional state, misperceptions, and bad data. Golfers of all levels make mental mistakes, but the better the player the fewer the mental errors. The better players have more resources to draw on: the experience from playing and practicing a great deal provides them with an accurate picture of their capabilities.

Some mistakes are purely mental and can be eliminated from your game just by thinking clearly. Some examples from personal experi-ence follow:

Choosing to pitch or chip a shot at a risky pin placement instead of getting the ball on the green and making two putts at worst.
Relying on yardage alone to select which club to hit to a green.
Hitting a drive with no specific target on the fairway to get the best angle to the pin.
Trying a shot on the course that you have not mastered in practice.
Gambling on a risky shot when it is not necessary.
Playing a shot over trouble when unnecessary.
Leaving the ball in a poor position such as a severe downhill putt or severe downhill lie when it could have been avoided.

All of these mistakes will cost you at least one shot per round. In a typical round, average golfers make the mistakes listed above at least once each time out. If they simply became aware and planned on thinking in terms of scoring and risk or reward options, they would shave at least five shots off their score without making one extra bad swing. If I had a magic training gimmick that would absolutely take five shots off your average game, golfers would be sending me money all day. This is not a gimmick but a guarantee: if your average score is 90 right now and you promise yourself not to make the mistakes I listed above, you will shave about five shots from your score from here on out (single-digit players and professionals may only shave one or two shots from their scores). Using your mind correctly is like getting free strokes every round.

Having a Game Plan

In every football game, the announcer will talk about each team's game plan. No coach can predict what is going to happen throughout the game or how the opposition will react. The coach with his assistants will analyze the field conditions and their own and the opponents' strengths and weaknesses and decide on the best options when situations present themselves. In golf, a similar game plan should be made before playing a round.

The reason for making a game plan is to make decisions in advance. In tournament play you may become nervous or preoccupied with your score, the weather may distract you from collecting good data, or unanticipated distractions may creep in such as having people come to watch you play. A game plan gives you an idea of what you want to do on every hole. You make the decisions while you are able to think clearly about the round in front of you rather than trying to come up with something in the heat of battle. A game plan takes a balanced approach to analyzing risks and rewards in advance. Is it smart to try for a birdie or would you be risking a double bogey by playing such a shot? The plan is not written in stone. It is a guide you construct while you are away from the course and it is based on your knowledge of the course in conjunction with your knowledge of yourself. If you had planned to hit a three-wood from a particular tee but get to that hole to find that the wind is against and a three-wood would not carry over some trouble, you are not bound to stick with your plan. You can change it.

The game plan is the overall guide, but on the course you must play in the process of the game itself. In other words, you play one shot at a time and one hole at a time while you are on the course. The plan is not an overall mandate for the round. Remember that you can only control the present. Feeling bad about the past or worried about the future are useless emotions both in golf and in life. They are emotions that operate best only in the present. You imagine feeling bad or guilty if you think of hurting someone's feelings or doing something against your personal values, so your mind tells you not to do it. When a physical or mental threat appears you become fearful in order to stimulate your fight or flight reaction so that you can deal with the threat. We misuse these emotions when we use them to try to control the past or future. The same thing is true in golf. Stay in the present and trust your mind to work on what is directly in front of you.

Know the Course

The first feature of smart play is to know the course as well as possible before playing it in a tournament. If it is your home course, do not take for granted that you know how to play every hole the best way. At my home course I always watch and ask the pro or the best players how they play a certain hole. The answers were not always the same but it gives me options to consider and fit to my own personal ability.

There is one hole on my home course that is particularly difficult. It is a par-4 dogleg hole that has out of bounds along the left side from the tee all along the hole. The landing area for a long iron or fairway wood is narrow; a driver will get you to a better entry place, but it requires a long and accurate drive. The green is severely pitched from right to left and is always fast. A pro told me to hit the driver because most of the trouble was nearer the tee and the hole opened up the farther that you hit it. Other players told me to hit a long iron or fairway wood to get the ball in play and then have a seven- to nine-iron shot left into the green.

To assess what would be best for me on this hole, I played the hole both ways in practice and ordinary rounds with my friends. From analyzing my abilities and the results that I achieved I developed a plan for myself that has worked well. I decided to hit a fairway wood or long iron to lay up if the tee markers were well back as I felt that I would have to hit a long and perfect drive to get over trouble and hit the fairway or area that opens. Like many players, I have a tendency to hook the ball when I try to get extra distance. The fairway wood or long iron pretty much guaranteed that I would be in play and have a short iron to hit into a tricky green. A par on this hole is a good score, so I would take it and move on with a smile on my face. On the other hand, if the tee markers were placed forward, as they are at times, I could hit a comfortable driver to the area that is open without fear of hitting out of bounds or into the trees. This scenario offered the chance to hit a pitching wedge into the green and presented a chance to make a birdie. My decisions may be adjusted because of wind, my ball striking on that particular day, or the situation in a match or tournament. The main thing is that I do have a plan in mind that was developed from collecting data and matching it to my own abilities. This is the essence of a game plan in miniature.

For each hole on the course try to develop a plan for yourself based on what is presented and how well you can handle the shots required. I try to break down a course by the pars. Here are some general guidelines:

Par-3s

- Always tee the ball up a little, as this allows you to create more spin; hit it high, and stop the ball on the green.
- Select a side of the tee that offers the best angle into the green. The middle of the tee is not always the best choice.

- Examine how the green best receives a ball. Is there a slope that will cause the ball to roll toward or away from a pin? Is there an area that will cause my ball to end up in trouble should I miss the green? Course designers love to have false fronts—collection areas that will funnel a ball off of the green and bunkers placed to tempt the risk taker on par-3 holes.
- If the par-3 is blind (you can't see the green from the tee), select a tree or marker in the distance to serve as an aiming point.
- Par-3s can be the hardest holes on the course but will not indicate it by the handicap rating on the scorecard. A par on a par-3 is a good score. A well-designed par-3 hole will not offer you an easy birdie chance.

Par-4 Holes

- What is the architect trying to do with the hole? Is he or she trying to tempt you into making a risky tee shot to lure you with a big reward of easy access to the green or are you asked to put a premium on accuracy over distance as a reward for placing your drive on the correct angle to the green?
- When practicing on the hole, select the part of the landing area that offers you the best approach to the green and make note of it in your book.
- Know the distances to any fairway bunkers. Determine whether you can carry them with your drive or whether you need to play away from them or hit short.
- If the hole is a dogleg, what distance is it to get in trouble should you hit it through the fairway? You should also note whether the fairway is hard, as the ball will run more. Note also if the fairway slopes in a way that will help or hurt your shot when it lands.
- Note how the green will receive a shot and figure out where the pins will likely be placed. Again, note bunkers and find a side of the green or an area in which it will be safe if you miss the green. This will allow you to make an easier up-and-down for par than missing the green in other areas near the green.

- Think of pin placements in terms of red, yellow, or green: Red means play to another part of the green because there is too much risk involved in going right at it. Yellow means go after the pin with caution and try to get it fairly close but do not risk a big number by going right at it. Green means go for the pin and try to make birdie. There is nothing protecting the pin and if you miss you can still make an easy par.

Par-5 Holes

- What overall scheme is the architect presenting? Is this a green that can be hit in two shots without much risk or is one that must be played in three shots to make sure you at least make a par?
- Par-5s are usually your best chance for making a birdie, so think a little more aggressively in devising your plan. For example, if you can hit the green in two or come close without risking hitting the ball into water, then go for it. If the hole is so long or hazardous that it takes three shots to get there, still think birdie. Plan your strategy so that your third shot is at the best angle to the pin and the distance is one that you are very comfortable with. Sometimes it is better to leave yourself with a 100-yard rather than a 50-yard shot to the pin, as the longer one may be more comfortable to you and offer the chance to hit the ball higher and stop it better than if you approach from the shorter distance.
- Do not automatically reach for the driver on a par five-5. The design of the hole may call for you to get the ball in play from the tee and then hit a long second shot. Often, architects set up par-5s in this manner and golfers fall into the trap of thinking that if it is a long par-5 they must hit a driver off of the tee. Everything that you think of doing on the first two shots on a par-5 is to set up where your third shot will be played. The third shot may be a putt for an eagle or an eight-iron at a good angle at the pin. Whatever the choice, everything is predicated on where the third shot will take place.
- Sometimes it becomes a par-6. There are some par-5 holes, particularly on newer courses, that are monsters. On one of my favorite

courses there is a par-5 that is over 600 yards long. The first time I played this hole, I hit a seven-iron for my third shot and made a birdie. The next time I played this hole the wind was howling and was dead against us. I hit a five-iron into the green on my fourth shot and two-putted for a "par"-6. This is simply adjusting the game plan to fit the situation. A bogey was a good score for that day, so make it a par-6 in your mind when a monster rears its head.

When you are evaluating a hole to develop your plan, you should look at it from different angles as well as getting information in the previously discussed ways. I like to look at a hole from the back of the green looking toward the tee. From this perspective you can see how the tee lines up with your desired landing spot. This is important because, many times, course designers will point you in the wrong direction with the tee on purpose. The older architects would do this as a subtle way of making a relatively easy hole a little tougher. Golfers who do not note this subtle little trick will wonder why they keep ending up in the rough or trees on one side every time they play the hole and hit seeming good shots from the tee.

When looking back from the green you may also get a better picture of how and from where your approach shot should be made. You will be able to see where the fairway opens and how it slopes. This may help you decide where to hit your drive. Many holes are designed so that an aggressive drive that is long will end up on a severe downhill lie. Golfers who love to blast the driver on every hole often fall into this trap and find that they are unable to hit a good shot from the lie that has been left to them.

As you look back, also note the contour of the green itself, as this will tell you what will happen once your ball lands on it, bounces, and rolls. This bit of information can be the difference between par or birdie, depending on where your ball lands. By looking at the contour of the green from the rear you can see the big picture and note the slopes around the green or where water would drain off it. This will give you great insight when it comes time to make putts on the green.

When you are already standing on the green and trying to read your putt from behind, you may not notice outside influences that cause breaks in the putt.

Every hole has a place where golfers walk off toward the next tee. This area usually has rough that is trampled down, so the grain will be against you as you play your ball. Note this area and make sure you avoid it, as the shot is very difficult to control. Also, note the depth of the bunkers around the green to see if they are places where it's okay to miss or ones from which it's very difficult to get the ball up and out.

Play Your Strengths

When you are making out a game plan for a course, know thyself. If you like to hit in from 150 yards rather than from 100, then play so that you give yourself that distance as much as possible. I played a round with our club champion, who hits a five-iron off of the first tee and the seven-iron into the green, as he feels comfortable in hitting a high shot that stops quickly. He knows the distance and feels that the advantage is his if he goes after the pin from that distance. Most players hit a fairway wood or driver and then play a wedge from a downhill lie to an undulating green. He made me rethink how I would play that hole from that day forward.

If you draw or fade the ball naturally, pick your spots to become aggressive. If you have a dogleg left hole and you draw the ball, then go ahead and start the ball down the middle and let it turn the corner. On the other hand, if you hit a fade, you must accept this hole as not fitting your game and play it to get your ball in a position to allow you to hit the ball onto the green with your second shot. There is no reason to try to turn the ball for a draw if your natural shot is a fade. Too many things can go wrong when you ask your mind to try something new or uncomfortable on the course. Similarly, if the pin is on the left side of the green and you hit a draw, you have a green light to start the ball in the center of the green and let it draw to the hole. If you fade, you need to start the ball at the pin and let it tail into the middle. The idea simply is to have a safe result should your ball (heaven forbid) go straight.

Playing to your strengths also entails knowing how well you play certain shots and how far you hit a particular club. If you have practiced and mastered a flop shot—one that is cut and lies almost straight up and lands softly—then by all means play it when the situation arises. If you do not have a flop shot in your arsenal, do not attempt one because it seems like a good idea for the shot in front of you. In this case, play to a safe area of the green and then take your two putts and get out of Dodge. This is smart golf that has saved you strokes even though you may have made a bogey. On a par-5 hole, do not try to hit a fairway wood automatically because you have a long way to the hole. If you hit your irons better than your fairway woods play two-iron shots rather than risk hitting a three-wood into the trees.

The distance to the pin is only one factor to consider. Distance is irrelevant if the green is elevated or well below where you are. It has little bearing on the club you select if there is a 30-mph wind at your back. A good player will always want to know what the distance is to the target but that is just the starting point in determining which club to hit. Since many things go into the selection of a club, I use a system that automatically factors in all the elements of the shot such as wind, wetness, or elevation.

I stand behind my ball and visualize hitting a pitching wedge toward the target and determine where the ball would land on the line. Then I visualize a nine-iron and note where that would land. I continue the process until I come to a club in my mind that brings me to the target with ease. It is my normal distance and not my career six-iron. Factoring in all the elements helps you "see" the shot rather than just getting a distance and equating it to a certain club. During practice, you should hit all your clubs so that you have a good idea how far each one carries. Try to lock that distance and flight pattern into your mind, as this will facilitate the visualization that you must do to get yourself thinking of the correct club for your shot.

Know When to Gamble

Lots of aspects of playing golf are fun, but one of the highlights of playing the game has to be making a decision to take a risk and then pulling it off. It is like the excitement and drama of a play at the plate in baseball. Taking a risk and ending up in trouble is frustrating and can cause self-doubt and a loss of confidence. Knowing when to gamble and when to play it safe is not only smart golf but also a receipe for emotional balance on the course.

I try to evaluate the risks and rewards of a hole in advance. Sometimes the risk is justified:

- If you are playing a match and your opponent is up on you and has already hit a good shot into a green near the end of the round. It is okay to go for broke and try to make a birdie and win the hole.
- If you come to a par-5 that you feel confident you can hit with a fairway wood shot. If you miss, you will still be in good shape to make a par. Only a poor shot will get you in trouble. For the skilled player this is not really gambling but simply being aggressive. This is how birdies are made; they come from a developed game and confidence in the execution of the shot. Playing reckless is totally different from being aggressive.
- If the shot fits your game. For example, if you hit a high wedge shot, you might go after a pin that is tucked close to a bunker rather than hitting it into the middle of the green and taking two putts. If a pin is tucked well to the right side of a green and you fade the ball then go after the pin as mentioned above. You are not really gambling recklessly when you place the odds in your favor.
- If in stroke play you are near the lead and can win with a good shot. Go for the shot that might allow you to win with the percentages on your side. Do not risk playing yourself out of the tournament, but take the risk into consideration and if the shot is inside you and you can visualize it—go for it.

Fairways and Greens

One thought that will never get you into trouble in managing a course is to think of hitting fairways and greens. This may seem obvious but how many players hit shots that they can't control and end up in trouble whether it was a drive or shot onto the green?

Think in terms of always keeping your ball in play and on the short grass. This does not mean that you have to steer the ball or control each shot by being overly cautious. This will only work against you. The thought "fairways and greens" helps you to focus on keeping the ball in places that will allow you to score well and help you avoid trouble. It is not a restrictive thought; rather, it should calm you and free you to expect good shots and know that you are capable of playing well by keeping your ball in good situations as much as possible.

Emotional Well-being

One facet of golf that is truly overlooked by most golfers aspiring to become good or great is the emotions that we both bring to and create on the golf course. When we discussed the types of thinking one category was "emotional management." Emotional management goes hand in hand with course management and is essential to playing well. We mentioned the mental or emotional states that separate Tiger Woods and Annika Sorenstam from the rest of us mere mortals. The point cannot be overstated that the emotional well being that you bring to and manage on the course is vital to your growth as a player.

The good player has confidence and self-esteem, brought about through practice, development, and achievement. Good players are happy with themselves knowing that they have been able to do well at a difficult task. The confidence that they have developed gives them a positive self-image as players. When they set up to play a shot they can clearly visualize what the shot will look like and what will happen. No worry or doubt creeps in to restrict muscles or cause the body to start to place controlling mechanics in place. The confidence is translated into trust. The player trusts his or her swing to look the way it was visualized and for the club to do what it was designed to do and the ball to fly the way it is supposed to as well. I read that when Tiger Woods was testing new golf balls, his criterion was that when he looked up he should see the ball exactly where he expected to see it. This is evidence of Tiger's mental ability to trust his swing and "know" what kind of results will be produced to the point that he has each shot implanted in his visual and sensory memory.

The Positive Golfer

Staying positive means recognizing that you have strengths, that you have had success, and that there is a tremendous potential inside you to become a great player. You need to be aware of your self-esteem and develop a positive sense of yourself as a golfer in order to move ahead in the game. Self-esteem helps us to manage ourselves effectively. If you come from the perspective that you are a good person and a good player and have great potential then you are coming from a position of strength. You are able to look at yourself and your emotions rationally and build on the ones that help you and correct the ones that are self-defeating. Self-esteem entails recognizing and celebrating your strengths and also recognizing that you have weaknesses and that you can accept and deal with them effectively. This is a healthy mind for golf and life.

The positive golfer has inner confidence that he or she can play well. Think of your all-time achievement round on your home course. Think of each hole and the best score you made on that hole. Go through your course hole by hole and then add up the totals of all your all-time achievement scores. The par at my home course is 70, but since I have played the course for 17 years, my all-time achievement round is 46. This would be a round that had six eagles and 12 birdies. Of course this would never happen at one time and in one round, but it represents the pinnacle of your golfing capability. You have already scored that on the course—just not all in one day. This potential lies within you; self-esteem is based on achievement.

Good golfers are not defensive. They are comfortable with themselves and their games. If someone points out a weakness in their game they are not upset. They know that golf is not a contest, and people who tease or criticize good players are probably jealous. Whatever the reason, what other people say or do is out of your control and does not call for any reaction as you are framed in self-worth and not self-doubt.

Positive golfers are proactive. They continually try to improve through practice, learning, lessons, and experimentation. They are always setting in place those things that challenge homeostasis in their golf world. They know that change is possible in both physical golf skills and emotional development on and off the course.

Learning and improving never stop but are a progression of continuing to get better by developing the strengths and diminishing the weaknesses. The positive golfer is not afraid to seek help by taking lessons, asking better players questions, or seeking advice from professionals in other areas such as psychology or nutrition if it will help them to become better. When good players practice, they relish the input that they get from good shots and see poor shots as a learning opportunity. By focusing on your strengths and successes, you create a neurochemical reaction in your brain that sends a pleasant sense of well-being and confidence through your whole body. Try smiling right now. You should experience a feeling of well-being. Your brain is not sure why you are smiling but it will send out some pleasant feeling because it knows that you are. This in turn translates into good golf.

Psychologists know that our emotions are hormonal in origin. Our brain produces hormones that will induce feelings of well-being if we train our minds to value ourselves as players and good persons. Positive self-talk such as congratulating ourselves after a good shot during practice or on the course is just one way of having our brains release positive hormones to help us feel good about ourselves. Tell yourself that that you are indeed capable of doing what you need to do to play well and your mind will help you accomplish that goal. Use affirmations or positive statements about yourself and your ability when you talk to yourself in practice and on the course. An affirmation may be "You have this shot," or "I know this putt is going in." Your brain will respond appropriately and will assist you in skillfully performing the task before you.

Self-defeating Behavior

You can see self-defeating behavior at work in golf and other sports. Letting anxiety make a player freeze over a shot or a putt is an example of a self-defeating behavior. Although an emotion is causing the behavior, it is the inability of the player to reduce, eliminate, or use the anxiety in a positive way that is the true problem. Players who let anger take over are defeating themselves as well. A player who is angry at himself is telling himself that he is no good and reinforcing it to others. We all have momentary lapses when we do not perform well and disappoint ourselves, but if we carry it to the point of anger, our brains load up on hormones that cause us to feel down and depressed after the anger subsides. In other words, the player who throws a temper tantrum on the course is probably cooked for the day. Put a fork in him, for he is done!

Self-defeating behavior causes the golfer to struggle on the course. The game loses its joy and becomes an unpleasant area of life. Once this occurs, the player loses that great desire to continue to learn and grow and become better. The National Golf Federation tells us that the golf population has stabilized in recent years at about 26 million golfers. The troubling part of this statistic is that 5 million to 10 million golfers leave the game every year, only to be replaced by new ones. People give up the game for various reasons. Many feel that golf takes up a lot of time, and this is indeed true. I did not play for 15 years while I helped raise my children and worked on my advanced degrees. I have the feeling, however, that many people leave the game out of frustration or in defeat. For them the game becomes a negative experience that produces anxiety or negative feelings and no longer is a recreational activity.

Many of these golfers could have learned to become better and enjoy the game had they taken a positive approach and sought to improve on a continual basis as outlined above. How you view yourself has everything to do with how well you perform. Practice so that your game steadily improves. And work, too, on being positive and building your self-esteem and self-worth.

CHAPTER FIVE

Scoring Well

GOLF IS A GAME OF SCORING WELL BY PLAYING SO THAT YOU TAKE FEWER strokes than your competitors. All strokes count the same: on your scorecard the 300-hundred-yard drive is equal to a two-foot putt. This means the ability to play well on the green is of heightened importance. There seems to be something intrinsically unfair about this when we look at it from that perspective. (Ben Hogan once advocated that putting had too much weight on the golf score and some form of adjustment should be made between full shots and putts.)

On the other hand, the greatness of the game lies in the fact that so many different skills are required to play it. Golf is a holistic endeavor that mandates both power and finesse; it forces us to think and evaluate and rewards those who possess not only the physical skills but also the analytical abilities needed to produce low scores. The fact that golf is not simply a long-driving contest allows the game to be played well by all. Many players who have made it to the very top of the game have done so through having great skill in scoring, which is somewhat independent of the ability to hit the ball very long or very accurately. Corey Pavin, Ben Crenshaw, and Brad Faxon are examples of players who have become outstanding mainly from short games—their ability to play well near and on the green.

Dave Pelz, the short-game guru of golf, made a stunning statement after examining the data he had collected from his television viewers: "If the average player who shoots an average score of ninety-two each round had Phil Mickelson or Annika Sorenstam finish their holes from one hundred yards each time despite what they did before to get there—their average score would be about seventy-five!"

The good news for you as a golfer who wants to make dramatic improvement is that your brain will allow you to learn the fine motor skills at a far greater pace and level of ease than a gross motor set of skills. In every basic psychology textbook there always seems to be a poster present entitled "How Your Brain Sees You." It shows a drawing of a man with body parts drawn to reflect the amount of the brain that is allocated to that part of the body. In the drawing the man's hands and eyes are enormously out of proportion. The poster's message is that approximately 40 percent of the human brain is allocated to our hands, the principal locus of fine motor control; and another 35 percent of our brain capacity is allocated to our visual sphere. Thus about 75 percent of our entire brain is devoted to eye-hand coordination.

This means that we can learn tasks associated with eye-hand coordination throughout our lives and that we can develop these skills no matter what our age. Children usually develop gross motor skills before the age of four—they have learned how to crawl, walk, jump, and run. At about this age, in kindergarten, we begin to put a crayon in a child's hand, as he or she is now ready to develop the fine motor skills. For the golfer, the short game is eye-hand coordination brought to life. The more you practice the short-game skills the more your brain builds links to help you learn and keep these skills. Some 60-year-olds who have never touched a golf club might have trouble learning to make a full swing, but the same person can learn to putt at a level that could approach a touring professional's—assuming a lot of time was given to practice and their commitment to learning was high.

If you look at course par as a score, on a par-72 course, 36 of the shots should come from putting alone. Most of the shots that we play are from 60 yards or less into the hole. It does not take a mathematician to realize that scoring well comes down to playing well in the short game. Wedge play, pitching, chipping, and putting are the shots that we play more than others and the ones that produce good or bad scores on our cards. On a par-72 course, you can expect to hit your driver about 12 times but your putter 36 times. Par allows us two putts per hole. You can never save a drive or make up a shot by hitting a better drive on the next hole. In putting, however, you can save a shot by one-putting on a green. You can get a shot back on the next hole after a bogey by one-putting for a birdie. The short game is where scores can soar or drop dramatically, compared to scores made on the shots hit from tee to green.

If you look at the PGA and LPGA Tour statistics, the longest drivers and even those who hit the ball onto the green in regulation at a higher percentage are seldom in the top ten in money rankings. Look at the top ten money winners and you will see players who do well in putting, sand saves, and up-and-downs. For several years I did a statistical analysis of the top ten money winners in a multiple correlation of various ranking of variables within their games. Time and again, the short-game skills predicted who would finish in the top ten with a 95 percent degree of accuracy.

Some golf writers have been quick to pick up on the fact that Tiger Woods is not among the top five players in distance off of the tee. Yet in 2003 he won more tournaments than anyone else and won tournaments at a 33 percent rate, meaning he won four out of 12 starts. Oh, by the way, the number one ranked player in putting this year: Tiger Woods.

In this chapter we will examine the thinking and skills necessary to execute well from 60 yards on in to the hole: wedge play, pitching, playing from bunkers, chipping, and putting. Our aim is to raise your awareness of how to become accurate and precise in the scoring aspects of the game. Putting will be discussed in even greater depth, as it is the area that truly levels the playing field, where brain can triumph over brawn and fine motor skills can match and take over from the gross motor skills when it comes to producing low scores. You will become convinced that the short game is the key area for dramatic improvement and that your practice and awareness on the course should be geared to this part of the game in proportion with its importance.

The importance to good scoring of being great around the green becomes clear to you when you actually analyze your round. Recently I played nine holes. Though I was not hitting the ball very well I shot even par 35—it seemed as if I should have had a higher score. When I analyzed my round, I saw that I had hit only three greens in regulation. I had made five up-and-downs with pitches or chips and one putt. I made one birdie and one bogey. This is a great example of what it takes to score. The best players in the world only hit about 12 greens in regulation per round. That means that on at least six holes, they will have to hit a wedge, pitch, chip, or sand shot to get a par. If they were not able to get up and down the vast majority of time, they would not keep their Tour cards very long. Only a few shots will separate the winner from a middle-of-the-pack player per round. Once you appreciate the importance of and then dedicate yourself to becoming confident in your short game, you can become a short-game master and get to the next level.

When I think about what makes good players different from average or poor golfers, the short game becomes very evident. I have often seen 25-handicap players hit drives 280 yards, not always consistently but often enough to see that they can hit the drive long and straight at least several times every round. I can honestly say that I have *never* seen a 25 handicapper hit a knock-down wedge and make it stop and spin. I have *never* seen a 25 handicapper hit a true flop shot, hit a long, low pitch shot that hits, then checks and rolls to the hole, or take under 30 putts in a round. I have seen single-digit players and professionals do the above many times in my life on a routine basis. The average touring professional will have about 28 putts per round. That is eight shots under what par allows. Imagine, keeping the very same game that you have but suddenly becoming as good a putter as the average touring professional. Without worrying about making one full swing, you could subtract at least eight shots from your score. Without doing a thing with your swing in one day you would go from being a 25 handicap to approximately a 15-handicap player. Of course, you will not be able to putt at a touring pro's level overnight, but I am not exaggerating when I say that attention to this area can lead to dramatic improvement in your handicap.

Wedge Play

The big difference in wedge play between the good player and the average one becomes more pronounced the closer the ball is to the green. The average golfer can hit a full wedge shot well enough to get onto the green from about 100 yards out. Once the distance becomes about 60 yards, the good and average players part company. The average player will try to control the distance the ball flies by taking the same setup and swing but just swinging easier into the ball. The good player controls distance by the length of the swing, not deceleration. The good player will hit the short shot with force while the average player will decelerate into the ball. The results speak for themselves: the player who decelerates into the ball has no real control over how far it flies and the attempt to slow down a long swing will lead to a host of poor shots, including hitting the ball fat, toeing it, or skulling it. The player who strikes the ball with a forceful, descending blow causes the ball to spin rapidly and get into the air so that it hits and stops on the green. The distance is plugged into the shot by the length of the backswing. The shorter you take the club back, the shorter the ball will fly. There is no need to guess at changing speeds; just change where you hold the club and how far you swing it back.

The simplicity of the forceful swing allows for the development of accuracy, and that is the main objective once you place a wedge in your hands.

The wedge is a precision instrument made to produce short, accurate shots. It is the heaviest club in your bag because the goal is to produce a repeating swing path that will follow gravity. The shaft is shorter to promote accuracy and control, the loft is high to allow the ball to get into the air quickly, and the club's bottom, or sole, has more bounce than the other irons in your bag. "Bounce" refers to the degree at which the back of the sole angles from front to back. The bounce allows the club to strike the ball first and then enter the turf and exit by gliding off of the ground. In other words, without bounce, the club would go into the turf and continue to bury itself on a path much like the lead edge of a shovel. Club makers have built a higher club face into the design to catch the ball in the grooves and place spin on the ball as it rides up the face. From this day forward, always think of a pitching, sand, or lob wedge as a precision instrument that is geared for accuracy. Do not be the guy who likes to tell everyone at the 19th hole that he hit a pitching wedge 150 yards to the green on some par-3 hole. Meanwhile, he will fail to mention that he shot 105 for the day.

The Setup

When playing a wedge from about 60 yards to the green, you must make some adjustments in order to accommodate for the shorter shaft of the club and the shorter backswing that you will make. These adjustments will make sense to you if you think of making a full swing with the long shaft of a driver and the shorter shaft of a pitching wedge. With the driver you have plenty of time to shift your weight to your back foot and then have the opportunity to shift onto your front side to receive your weight so you can swing through while your weight is set for you. With the driver, you have time as well to turn and clear your hips out of the way while your arms swing through impact. With the short backswing and short shaft of the wedge, it would be almost impossible to make some quick action to get the hips out of the way in time for your arms to flow through the impact area.

In order to make a good wedge shot, make these adjustments as you practice and then take them to the course:

- Place most of your weight on your front foot. This will allow you to be balanced as you come into impact and through to your finish. You will not have time to shift your weight to the back foot and then onto the front, so just pre-set it onto the front foot and leave it there for the entire swing.
- Open your stance slightly by pulling your front foot back from the target line about three to five inches. Open your toe at about 45 degrees toward the target for balance.
- Choke down on the handle of the club to shorten your backswing and give you more control over the shot. By choking down on the

grip, you shorten the club itself. You can swing with force but the ball will naturally go a shorter distance.

- Place your shoulders parallel to your target line, as this ensures an accurate aim.
- Stand a little closer to the ball and let your arms hang from your shoulders. Naturally align to the line that they make toward the target.
- Tilt your hands forward of the ball and play it toward the middle or slightly right of the middle of your stance. This will make sure that you contact the ball with a descending blow that is led by your hands.

These are the mechanical fundamentals of a wedge shot. As you practice, always review these and set up using all the above elements to help you hit great wedge shots every time. The wedge game is based on creativity and precise settings. You must develop your wedge shots in practice in order to learn the mechanics and feel of the shot and also to learn how to produce the proper flight and distance that you need for the shot.

During practice, learn to equate where your hands are in the backswing to a certain distance. Use the idea of a clock face to set your distance to a particular length. For example, if the ball is at six, swing your hands back to seven and strike the ball and see how far it flies; move to up to eight, then nine and note the distances that each "setting" produces. The speed of the backswing and downswing never changes. The difference in distance depends only on the distance your hands move back and forward. A good way to practice your distance control is to use the clock-face method to gradually bring you to targets that are progressively farther away. Then, start bringing the ball back by hitting it shorter distances until you are hitting the ball about ten yards. When I work with Sandra Palmer, she has me do this drill to learn the feel for this shot. She was trained by Harvey Pennick, who was the advocate of such practice for feel and control.

On the Course

When you come to a wedge shot on the course, look at the target while taking different lengths of swings. Try to feel the swing that matches the distance and dial it into your clock system. Set up to the ball as spelled out above and fire at the pin with confidence. If you watch the touring pros on television, you will see that they may make one practice swing before a full shot just to loosen their muscles. On a wedge, pitch, or chip shot, you will see them make practice strokes over and over. They are not practicing the swing; they are simply trying to find the swing that will produce the desired flight and distance. Once they find it, they may make several rehearsals to make sure that they have the correct setting dialed into their minds. Follow their example by sensing the distance and then drawing on the memory you developed in practice of how far back you should swing. Make some swings so that you can "feel" the distance and visualize the shot that you want. Visualize your clock-face position for the length of backswing, take a few rehearsal swings, and then fire at the hole.

Visualization is important to your whole game and especially in the short game. The ability to "see" the kind of shot becomes critical because the short game requires shots that are different from a full shot in the length of the swing, the flight of the ball, and the reaction of the ball on the green. I believe that the ability to visualize the type of shot needed to get the ball close and to transfer the image from your mind to a swing is the key ability of great short-game players. You should work hard in practice to visualize your wedge shot flying and stopping at a particular target and then make a swing that produces that shot for real. If you do this every time you hit a short shot, you will be building links and rewiring your brain to build visualization skills that will tell your body what to do during the swing. The more you do this kind of practice the better you will become at making the transfer from what your mind sees to what your swing produces.

When you practice with a partner, try to have a competition to hit to targets of different lengths with your pitching wedge. For every shot in the competition, make a swing and visualize the shot, then make a rehearsal swing to get your setting. Finally, set up to the ball correctly and make your shot. You will notice that you will become incrementally better and better over a relatively short span of time. Never hit a wedge without seeing the shot first or you will be exercising only your muscles instead of training your mind as well.

Since the wedge is a precision instrument, all your emphasis should be on accuracy. Stand behind your ball and pick out a spot in front of your ball along the target line to use as a guide. Hit the ball so that it flies over that spot. From behind the ball determine the ball flight that you will need. If you need to hit it high and land it soft play the ball more forward in your stance so you will still hit down on the ball but your divot will be more shallow and the ball will hit higher on the face and fly higher into the air.

The placement of my hands on the grip depends on the distance I need to hit the ball. The more you practice the more able you will be to know how far to choke down on the club. It will be automatic for you to choose your setting after you have hit a number of shots. When you swing back always feel your wrists cock up to a 90-degree angle created by your left arm and the shaft of the club at the finish of your backswing. For example, if your setting is nine o'clock, you should swing back so that your hands are in line with your toe line and are about waist-high and the club head is pointing straight up. Never cock your wrists more than 90 degrees as this will cause you to lose the feeling of starting down from a solid position. When you start down with the wedge, you should feel as if you are coming down on the ball in a steep manner and pinching it out of the turf. Feel as if you start doing this by pulling your hands down in one unit. Your hands will release naturally from the weight of the club. Always make sure to strike the ball first on the downswing as this is the key to great wedge shots that fly with accuracy.

If you need to keep it low, such as in high-wind conditions, play the ball back in your stance, bring the club upright so that you come into it at a steep angle, and follow through by holding the club low as well. You should finish with the club head pointing at the target. This is often called the knockdown shot and it is used by many skilled players on a regular basis. The knockdown wedge keeps the ball out of the air so that it is not subject to any wind; it will not bounce and roll once it lands but will hit, bounce once, and then spin back. This shot is great for accuracy because it removes variables such as wind and the texture of the green. Sergio Garcia hits this shot on almost every wedge shot that he has and is the master of getting the ball up and down when he has a wedge in his hands.

Practice the knockdown shot, as it will lower your scores dramatically once you can rely on it on the course. The feeling of hitting the knockdown is different from that of a full shot. There is a sense of holding your wrist firm as you go through impact. The right hand does not roll over after impact but holds the club face straight into the ball at impact and keeps it there in the abbreviated follow-through. Your hands release the club but do not open or close the club face as you would see in a normal full swing with an iron. Practice this shot so that you strike the ball crisply and send it on a straight line drive to the pin. If you have trouble getting the intricacies of this shot down, have your pro give you a half-hour lesson just on knockdown. He or she will watch you to make sure that you are making the correct move with the wedge for this shot. It is well worth the time and effort to learn this shot as it is the gravy shot for most good players.

The Pitch Shot

The pitch shot is a shot that gets the ball into the air, lands on the green, and settles near the pin. Some players have called it a mini-golf swing. I do not like this thought as it leads to making a weight shift or rotating your forearms as the club swings. I use a setup and swing that simplify the shot and will produce incredible accuracy for you. When I teach this method, students are able to learn it quickly and to become deadly accurate with very little practice. The difficult part is learning the feel or distance control necessary. This will come with practice.

The Setup for a Pitch Shot

To set up to hit a short shot that gets into the air and lands straight at the target, you should choose a lofted club such as your sand wedge or pitching wedge. I prefer the sand wedge as it glides over the turf and slides through the rough nicely. For pitching, it is a good idea to practice with one club over and over. You will always use this club on the course. You will gain a feel for how far you need to swing the club back and forth and you will get your distance setting dialed in as you practice with just the one club.

Stand so that your feet are under your shoulders for good balance but place most of your weight on your front foot and leave it there as you would for your shorter wedge shots. Your stance should be slightly open with your shoulders creating a line toward the target and the lead edge of the club face pointing there as well. I grip the club in the middle of the handle or three quarters up the handle. Try to avoid gripping too far down toward the shaft as this may cause you to get the club back too fast and flip it forward. You want to feel the club head swinging in your hands for control. The sand wedge is the heaviest club in your golf bag and will provide that feeling.

Here I depart from what most golf instructors teach. I got this technique from watching the professionals play up close and talking to them about the shot. They would never consider the pitch shot a mini-golf-swing, as that would incorporate too many extraneous elements. The pitch shot is a feel shot that benefits from simplicity and trust. Keep the fundamentals and mechanics simple and then trust your body to execute the shot. Here is how I execute my pitch shot:

- Stand behind the ball and sight down the target line. Select the spot on the green where you want your ball to land to allow it to bounce and roll to the hole. Select a spot on the target line about one foot in front of your ball as an aiming point. Move to the side of the ball and make several rehearsal swings while looking at the spot on the green where you want the ball to land. Visualize the flight of the ball, the landing, and the release to the hole. Try to see it go in the cup. Make a perfect shot in your mind; this helps your mind send great signals to your muscles.

- Step up to the ball so that it is slightly to the right of the middle of your stance.
- Here is the part that is different. Break your wrists back almost from the start of the backswing until they are cocked or at not more than 90 degrees. The wrists simply hinge back while your arms just swing back a little. From the end of the backswing and into the ball and beyond there is no breaking or turning of the wrists. You simply hold your wrists firm so that the club face is held square at impact and beyond. The club head should only slightly pass your hands in the follow-through. Your wrists are firm but not stiff as you get the feeling of taking the club straight back and then sending it straight along the target line with the face "looking" at the target the whole way. It is almost impossible to hit the ball left or right of your target using this method as you would have to manipulate something in order to do so. It is so simple that you will amaze yourself at the results.

Find a practice area that has a green that you can pitch to. Try the method of breaking the wrist back with a little arm movement and then holding your wrists firm and hitting the ball straight at the target. The distance the arms swing back depends on the length of the pitch shot. If it is 40 yards, then you must make a good arm swing back, but the secret is holding the wrists firm through impact and beyond. The club will do all the work, as it is designed to glide off the turf and get the ball into the air. Never try to scoop it up. Trust hitting the ball with firm wrists in practice to learn the shot and then develop feel for distance by increasing the length of your backswing and follow-through.

The most common fault that I have seen in poor pitch shots occurs when a player takes a long backswing and then decelerates into the ball. The result is usually a stubbed shot—one that lands well short of the target. Feel committed to the shot in your mind and accelerate the club through impact in order to let the club do its work and to hit crisp shots that land on your spot. Your rehearsal swings should reflect an accelerated swing that is not tentative and a mind-set that is totally confident in your ability to make the shot happen. This shot is well within your ability. Learn it in practice, use it on the course under pressure, and it will be yours for your golfing lifetime. Within a short time, your scores will start going down as a result of being able to get the ball up off the green and to one-putt for a par when in the past you had to settle for a bogey almost every time you missed a green.

You should try to practice pitch shots from different types of lies so that you adjust to different kinds of grass, uphill or downhill slopes, greens that slope away or toward you, and learn how much stop or spin you normally get with your pitch shots. This type of practice gives you feedback that will come in handy when you go to the course. Once you hit pitch shots that consistently fly straight to the target, make subtle changes to produce the type of flight and amount of carry and spin that best suit you.

On the green you are always gathering information to help you. Watch how your playing partners' shots hit and land on the green. Did they check up quickly or bounce and roll after they landed? Was there a lot of break near the hole? Did the green seem fast or slow? All these things are information that will help you plan your shot. This information allows you to plan your shot, visualize it, and then execute it with confidence. We will discuss confidence more in depth when we get to the section on putting. Confidence is the gatekeeper of good performance around and on the green. If you have real confidence your mind will allow your muscles to perform as you want them to. If you lack confidence, it is as if you have no chance other than luck of making a good shot. Always remember to build your confidence in order to pass through the gate to great play.

The Pitch and Run

Every time a Ryder Cup is played, we can clearly see the contrast of play between the Americans and Europeans. The most obvious difference comes in the short shots near the green. The Europeans, who are used to playing in bitter winds and hard, sandy turf, use the bump-and-run shot very often. American professionals, who are used to soft, fast greens, tend to throw the ball to the pin and spin it to a stop. The Europeans seem to have a distinct advantage in this area, as the bump-and-run shot can be played in almost every situation with good results once it is learned. It also is a shot that can be used to get at particularly difficult pins with a minimum of risk.

Use the bump-and-run to land the ball off the green and have it bounce and roll onto the green. If the pin is located close to the front you can use the bump-and-run to hit the ball into a slope or rough in front of the green to kill the speed and then have it hop up onto the green. A normal pitch or chip would land on the green and run too far by the hole. Play the ball from a position in the middle of or back in your stance and keep your wrists firm through impact to ensure accuracy.

The bump-and-run shot is played with a swing that goes straight back and through in almost a pendulum motion. The club is kept low both going back and through to make sure the ball stays down. The ball should fly like a low-line drive, hit, bounce, and roll to the target. You can use a four-iron up through seven-iron to get the job done.

The bump-and-run can be a great shot when you are faced with some difficult situations around the green. One situation that always seems to come into play during a round is when you have a steep slope in front of you to an elevated green with the pin fairly close to you. There are only a few options available to you and the easiest to execute is the bump-and-run. If there is not heavy rough on the slope, you may hit the shot so that the ball climbs the hill and rolls onto the green. The secret is to hit the bump-and-run so that it lands before the bottom of the slope and then begins to bounce and roll. Many players try to slam a ball into the side of the hill and hope for a good bounce. This is very tricky and depends too much on luck. If you hit the ball firmly so that it is rolling at the bottom of the slope it will roll up the slope and lose speed as it gets closer to the green. The perfect shot hits the green as it is losing its speed and rolls nicely to the pin.

This shot is well within an average player's capability and is much easier than trying to cut a wedge shot into the air. Practice the bump-and-run on level ground until you can find and dial in your distance with consistency. Then, find a place on your course to practice the shot by hitting it near the base of the slope and letting it track up the hill and onto the green. This shot is a stroke saver that you will love to have in your repertoire.

Another use for the bump-and-run is when you are faced with a severe downhill pitch shot. It is very difficult to hit a shot that gets up into the air and lands softly from a severe downhill lie near the green, for several reasons: your swing is not fast enough to produce much spin; the tendency is to de-loft the club because of the slope; and the most common error comes from hitting the ball in the middle or skulling it over the green. The bump-and-run shot offers you the opportunity to control the shot much better. You can make a short back-swing and strike down on the ball to bump it down the slope with good contact and get it rolling toward your target. One law of golf physics that you should put in your memory bank is that a rolling ball has a much greater chance of going into the hole than a bouncing ball. At every opportunity around the green, get your ball down and rolling as soon as possible if the situation allows you to.

The Lob Shot

Golfers are always amazed to see good players hit a shot that seems to go almost straight up into the air and then land softly and stop near the hole. Phil Mickelson has made this shot famous because of his skillful execution in seemingly impossible situations. The lob shot offers you a chance to get the ball close when no other shot will work. When faced with hitting a ball over a bunker to a pin cut close to the other side of the bunker, most golfers simply hit a shot to the middle of the green and take two putts. This is great strategy in that you know what shots you have and you are playing it smart in taking a bogey and moving on rather than making a big number. But if you learn the lob shot, you will have a technique to hit the ball up into the air and get it near the pin for a par.

The lob shot is a risky shot because the swing has a great deal of speed for a ball to travel a short distance. I feel that most golfers never attempt this shot for that very reason. If you miss the shot and catch the ball thin or square on the face, it will fly well over the green and usually into trouble. The shot is relatively easy to pull off once you practice and get a feel for how to do it. You must remove the fear factor by hitting hundreds of these shots with force so that it becomes automatic. Conquer the fear and you have a shot that will save you strokes and save you shots.

One time in South Carolina a teaching professional friend of mine asked me to demonstrate the lob shot to four players in his golf school class. My shots to various targets went well into the air and landed on the green like a dead quail. When we demonstrated the technique, none of the amateurs could hit it at all. They simply refused to let themselves swing with the force needed to get the ball up and into the air. They lacked confidence and let fear prevent them from swinging at a speed that felt way too hard for the distance to the target. This was an assault on their homeostasis.

The mechanics of the lob shot involve opening your stance to about 45 degrees to promote an outside-to-in swing, placing your weight on the front foot and leaving it there, and opening the face of the wedge so much that it almost lies flat on the ground. The lead edge of the wedge points at the target while your feet are angled well to the left. Your shoulders are also pointed well to the left to allow the outside-to-in swing. The key is to have the lead edge pointed directly at the target, as this is the direction the ball will fly. Use a lofted wedge such as a 60-degree or a lob wedge. Swing back by taking the club to the outside of the target line and then down so that it comes in across the target line and comes under the ball and keeps moving. Hold the club so that the face stays well open and does not roll closed at impact. Swing much harder than you would ever expect, using a force about three times that of normal. As long as your club face remains wide open, the added speed of the swing causes the ball to go high into the air and not forward. You should get the feeling of cutting the legs from out from under the ball as the wedge slides under. The ball comes in contact with the open club face and shoots straight up into the air.

The lob shot begs you to practice it so many times that all fear is gone and your level of confidence is such that you do not even hesitate to use the shot on the course. Try to find a practice area that has a bunker and a green behind it. Set up as explained above and practice hitting the lob shot over the bunker so that it stops on the green. The bunker will force you to cut the ball into the air or you will dump it into the sand. Trust yourself to accelerate the swing so that the force sends the ball up. To vary your distances, just close the face a little. You can start by opening the face from being almost flat on the ground, for a shot that will travel only a few yards, to closing it to about 45-degrees, to hit the ball about 30 yards. Experimentation will help you find your distance settings for this shot. This shot is an essential part of great players' games. Vijay Singh always ends his daily practice sessions by hitting quite a few lob shots, both to keep his confidence level high for this shot and also to help him develop feel and promote fine motor development.

The Chip Shot

The chip shot is used when you are close to the green and you need to hit the ball into the air a short way and then have it roll. Set up to the shot as if you were hitting a putt. Use your putting stance and even your putting grip. The swing should be like that of a putter as well, as there is little or no movement of the wrists or body. Use a club with loft such as a six-, seven-, or eight-iron; your putting stroke will remain the same but the loft of the club will lift the ball a short distance without any lifting action on your part. Swing back and forth in a pendulum motion, and then all you need to do is make contact with the ball in a downward motion just where the ball meets the ground. Trust the club to loft he ball onto the green. The club is designed to do this, so just trust it.

The chip shot should land on the green and get rolling as soon as possible to the hole. The ball should have no back or side spin but should land and then roll straight. You will read the green for the chip shot in the same way you would for a putt. Play the ball about in the middle of your stance, or where you would normally place the ball for your putts. Feel as if you are making a stroke with no flipping of the wrists. For longer chips, you may have a little bend or break in your wrists, but let it come naturally and do not consciously try to break your wrists back and forth.

The chip shot differs from other shots in that while you have a line to the hole in mind, your target is a landing spot and not the hole. You must pick a spot where you feel the ball will land and then roll to the cup. A basic rule of thumb to start with is to hit the ball so that it flies about one third of the way to the hole and rolls the other two thirds. Of course, modify this as you develop your chipping stroke and adjust for the speed and slope of the green.

The key to becoming a great chipper is to seek perfection. Whether you are practicing or have the shot on the course, try to have the ball go into the hole. This does not mean to hit every chip well beyond the hole but strike it with the correct distance control as set by the length of your backswing. I have read instruction books and articles that tell the reader to chip to an imaginary three-foot circle. This like telling a student to aim for an 80 in a test instead of 100.

If you try to make every chip go into the hole when you practice, you will be setting a high bar for yourself and you will refine your skills to a higher level than if you settle for a three-foot circle. Some psychologists think that the latter attitude may cause the player to be practicing missing; but I view it from a different perspective. Even though you will not make every chip or even close to the majority of them, by chipping to make the ball go into the hole you are making your mind build links to help you process the chip shot at a higher level. It forces you to focus in practice and never get sloppy. If your goal is to become better, practice to a three-foot circle. If you want to become great, practice to hit the hole with every shot.

The thing that seems to hurt most golfers most often on chip shots is excess movement. Keep your eyes focused on the back of your ball and take your stroke back and through. After you have struck the ball, keep your eyes on the grass that was under the ball. Look up only when you hear the ball land on the green. If you come up too soon or slide forward with the club, you will hit the ball thin or fat. Your intermediate objective is to make solid contact. Once you have done that, you have done your part in getting the ball on the way to the hole. Place your weight forward and keep it there as a brace for the shot. You must keep your weight off the back foot for a chip shot. In fact, I have seen pros practice with their back foot lifted off of the ground, and some players even lift most of their heel off the ground when they play during an actual round.

I mentioned "solid contact" as an intermediate objective in the chip shot. An objective is something that you must do in order to reach your goal. A child has to learn how to pronounce consonant blends such as "br" before he or she can learn to pronounce the word "bring." In the same way, you must make solid contact in order to hit chip shots that may drop into the cup. During practice you might start by staying still over the ball, using the eyes drill above, and simply hitting chips solidly without worrying where they end up. All your focus is given to making solid contact with the club and ball. Make swings back and forth with your eyes on the back of the ball and listen for the ball to land before you look up. You have no target and no pressure except to make clean contact. I emphasize this drill for chipping and putting because I am convinced that most chips and putts are missed because they are not hit properly, rather than because they have been misread. This will become more evident when we discuss putting. Move the ball around in your ball position to find the exact spot where your club strikes the ball with a slight downward blow (this varies from player to player). This is your ideal ball position for chipping.

Many players ask whether they should leave the pin in while they chip from off the green. There are two schools of thought on this question. Studies by golf magazines and others have found that more balls will go in if you leave the pin in the cup. The pin will tend to stop a ball and deliver it downward into the hole. On the other hand, some players feel that the pin causes the ball to bounce off it and away from the hole. Lee Trevino once said, "A pin that is left in will only help a bad shot."

Many players take the pin out as it gives them the mental picture of making the ball go into the hole much as a putt would drop into a hole without a pin. It makes them feel more aggressive and puts them in a good mind-set for making the chip.

My own advice is always to leave the pin in the cup for a downhill chip and take it out for an uphill one. In this way, the pin will prevent a rolling chip going down a hill. On an uphill chip, the back of the cup is higher so you already have a backstop and you do not need the pin. I like to leave the pin in on fast greens as the tendency on such greens is to err in hitting the chip too fast rather than too slow. I take the pin out on slow greens as you need to hit the ball more aggressively to the hole and removing the pin might help. Use what you feel is best for you based on your own experience and the information presented here.

Putting from off the Green

When the fairway grass is mowed to a very short length, hitting a pitch or chip shot may become difficult as there is little room for error. There is always the chance of stubbing the club behind the ball, or "chilly-dipping" the shot. In this case you may be better off putting the ball from off the green. This has been called the "Texas wedge" because of the lack of grass in the Texas summer and the high winds that frequently occur in that state, but more generally it is called a putter. A putter is easy to get rolling on the ground and you eliminate the stubbed shot or the danger of wind catching your ball.

To putt from off the green, you must examine the ground along the line of your shot. Never putt through a patch of rough or long grass, an area that is bumpy, or one that has a lot of slope. It simply becomes too tricky. If you have a fairly level line to the pin on short-mown grass that is smooth, then by all means putt the ball. Use your normal putting stroke but grip the putter a little more firmly than usual in order to make sure you hit it with enough velocity to have it travel over the fairway grass.

You also need to look at the grain of grass that you have in front of you on the fairway when putting. If the grass is shiny, the grain is flowing toward the hole and your ball should roll smoothly. If the grass is dark green the grain is against you and the ball may pop up and bounce as it fights the tops of the grass blades. If the grain is severe, such as you would find with Bermuda grass, you might opt not for putting but for pitching the ball over this kind of grain. If the grass sets up straight, then putt the ball. Read the break in the fairway grass as you would read the break on the green.

Playing from Hardpan

Around each green there always seems to be an area of hardpan—dirt that is packed down with little or no grass. To play from this area, you may putt the ball if there is no heavy grass or other problem between your ball and the green. If you cannot putt the ball, take a low-loft club such as a four-iron and chip the ball by clipping it off the dirt. A lofted club will have too much bounce and might cause you to skull or blade the shot over the green.

Playing from Rough Around the Green

A common design feature of modern courses is rough around the green with a ring of fringe. This presents us with several problems that we need to learn how to respond to. If your ball is in fairly deep rough (three to five inches) do not try to chip or putt out of it as the grass will stop your club or come between the club and the ball. Your best bet is to pitch the ball from the rough by laying the ball in the middle of your stance and making a swing that allows your sand wedge to slide under the ball and lift it onto the green. You must allow for some roll as the grass will take any spin from the ball.

If the ball is setting up fairly well in the rough, you may opt to use a fairway wood to hit the shot. Tiger Woods has made this shot popular as he uses it regularly to get the ball onto the green nicely. Golf historians tell us that this kind of shot was used as far back as the 1920s, but Tiger's popularity has made it famous. To hit this shot, place the ball slightly forward of the middle of your stance and make a putting or chipping stroke with a minimum of wrist movement. The fairway wood will glide on top of the grass behind the ball and not get caught up in it, like an iron. The fairway wood has considerable loft so the ball will get into the air easily and then roll once it lands on the green, much as would a chip shot. This is a fun shot that you can learn quickly. If you can chip and putt fairly well, then you can learn this shot by using the same stroke and trusting the loft to lift the ball. Try using a three-wood or five-wood to see which club gives you the best feel for hitting the shot. Keep your hands forward and choke down toward the shaft for control.

The Sand Shots

Every course uses sand traps, called bunkers, around the green as hazards that punish bad shots. To get out of bunkers you need a repertoire of sand shots. On sand shots you hit behind the ball. It is the one class of shots in golf that you never really hit the ball with direct contact with your club face. The basic sand shot is not very difficult to play, once you learn how to execute it. In fact, many touring professionals opt to hit the ball into a bunker rather than the rough, as the bunker shot can be easier to control and more predictable. In this strategy, the player aims so that if the approach shot misses, such as on a long par-5, only a simple bunker shot is left to get the ball close. The basic sand shot almost guarantees the touring pro an up-and-down. The challenge in the sand comes from difficult lies that may be buried, downhill, or uphill on wet or fluffy sand or in bunkers with steep lips, as we see in the European courses.

Most bunkers are shaped so that once a ball lands in one, it is funneled to the middle, a relatively flat area that offers a good chance to get the ball up and out. Familiarize yourself with different types of sand and with the type used on a specific course and prepare yourself to play from them. The two main types of sand are coarse and fine. Coarse sand calls for a shot that strikes closer to the ball and travels a short distance under the ball. Select a sand wedge that has less bounce and a narrow flange in order to deal with this type of sand better. On the other hand, if you are playing a course that has fine, fluffy sand, as you often find in Florida, you will need to hit farther behind the ball with a wedge that can glide through more sand while going deeper. In this case, opt for a wedge that has more bounce and a bigger flange on the sole. You can test the sand in a practice bunker or even venture out on the course and look at it to get a good idea of what you will need.

Not only do you not actually hit the ball in the sand shot, but it is also the one shot where you do not look at the ball while you are playing it. This may sound troublesome but it is actually easier than it appears. The ball is lifted out of the sand when the club is passed under it; the sand is thrown forward and the ball is spun backward and lifted into the air from the spin. The club enters the sand behind the ball, slides under the ball, and then exits on the other side as the displaced sand is thrown forward.

The club to execute this shot, the sand wedge, was invented before World War II by the great Italian-American golf champion, Gene Sarazen. Mr. Sarazen got his idea from the design of an airplane's wing, which is designed to produce lift. He turned the design around to produce the opposite effect: a shape that would dig and then glide off of a surface then come up without getting stuck. The sole of the sand wedge forms an angle that increases from the front (the leading edge) to the rear, or flange. The result is that the club enters the sand fine but the bounce, or angle, added to the back forces the club to stop digging and to start gliding straight ahead once it hits the bottom. The design feature called bounce has been on sand wedges ever since, and most irons today have some degree of bounce to help them play well from the fairway.

The Basic Sand Shot

There are two methods to hit a basic sand shot from a greenside bunker. If you are a higher-handicap player, your bottom line is to make sure you get the ball out and fairly close every time. Set up to the ball with your feet just slightly open and keep your club face square to the target. Make a routine pitching swing and strike the sand a few inches behind the ball; make sure that you follow through. The ball will come out, land, and roll more than other sand shots, but the important thing is that you are out of the bunker and on the green. In seeking improvement, you might start with this shot if you are playing in the nineties and want to get into the eighties. Once you have mastered this shot, which is very simple, you may move up to the type of sand shot used by the pros.

The professional golfers and low handicappers want to hit the ball not only to get it out of the bunker but also so that it flies up and out of the bunker, spins to a stop, and rolls just a little bit to the pin. In order to do this, they open their stance very wide, swing on an outside-to-in plane, and cut across the sand behind the ball to finish with a good, aggressive follow-through. They break their wrists early and get the club into the air quickly on the backswing and then hit down and through with force to send the sand flying out and the ball spinning at a high rate.

Here are some guiding principles of dos and don'ts in sand play:

- Always look at the point where you want your club to enter the sand behind the ball, not at the ball. Your eye-hand coordination must be directed to hitting the sand behind the ball to allow the club to slide under it. Mr. Sarezen designed the club to make sand shots easier. Trust the club to do its job by letting it enter the sand and then have the bounce glide under the ball. If you try to hit the ball, scoop the sand and ball into the air, or slam the sand behind the ball with a closed face, you are doomed to leave the ball in the bunker.
- Dig your feet into the sand. There are several reasons for this. (1) So that you will not slip or lose your balance while swinging. Once

you dig in with your feet, take a backswing or practice swing without touching the sand to feel whether your stance is secure. (2) By digging into the sand with your feet you get to test the texture of the sand without breaking any rule of golf. As you wiggle your feet into the sand, see if the sand gets hard just under the surface, which is common in many northern courses that have tough winters and use a covering of sand over hard-packed sand in their bunkers. (3) Dig in to lower your body, for with the sand shot you want to go under the ball, unlike shots that hit the ball off of the level surface by direct contact. One common fault that many amateurs make is to dig their feet into the sand so deeply that they have lowered themselves to a point where it is almost guaranteed that they will stick the club into the ground behind the ball and leave it there. I think this comes from watching the professionals take care in setting their feet in the bunker and misinterpreting it to mean the deeper you go the better. Only dig in to lower your body to the amount that you want to slide under the ball.

- Keep your weight evenly distributed on both feet. Play the ball slightly forward in your stance and keep your hands behind the ball at address in order to avoid shutting the face down.
- The more you open the face, the shorter and higher the ball will fly. As you close the face, the longer and lower the ball will travel.
- The feeling of a good sand shot is one of "thumping" the sand so that a slab of it is cut from the bunker just under the ball.
- Keep your grip in a neutral position so that you do not roll your left hand over at impact. When you finish your swing, the face of the sand wedge should be pointing up as if you were serving a glass on it. This ensures that you did not close the face but let it stay open throughout the swing in order to have the bounce work through the sand.
- Your mental picture is slow and easy. Many touring pros have said that they walk slowly into the bunker and hold the club lightly in their hands to remind themselves to swing smoothly with no

hurried motion. My all-time favorite teaching pro was the former touring professional Toby Lyons. Toby's swing thought for hitting sand shots was "Throw sand on the green." If you throw sand on the green when hitting sand shots it is almost impossible to leave the ball in the bunker. To this day I use Toby's swing thought for every bunker shot.

- Your mental approach is vital to playing well from the sand. View it as an opportunity to display your skills. Practice will remove any fear, for once you learn the sand shot it is easy to reproduce it on demand. Take a few practice swings from outside the bunker and stand behind the ball to visualize your shot and see how the contours of the green may affect the bounce and roll. Try to see your ball flying to the hole, stopping, and nestling close to the pin. Breathe deeply to oxygenate your brain and muscles and let a feeling of calmness take over your body. The sand-shot swing is a flowing, smooth one that builds speed gradually and is beautiful when executed well. Feel as if you are in slow motion as you walk to your ball and set up. Swing along your body line and simply let the club do the work. When we start to interfere with the flow of the swing, we cause the problems that result in skulled and fat shots. Your mind knows how to execute the shot from practice. Just turn the shot over to your mind and let it happen. This is a wonderful time to get out of your own way.

- Swing the club upright in the backswing and down and through as you go through impact with the sand. Never try to stop the club in the sand hoping the ball will pop out. The most common fault among all players who miss a bunker shot is decelerating or slowing down as the club comes down and through the sand. The swing has to be about three times harder than what you would normally use to hit a ball the same distance. The sand will slow the club and allow for the shorter ball flight. You set the distance on sand shots by the length of your follow-through. Make sure that you make a shoulder turn, as the sand shot cannot be made with just the arms and hands.

- On fairly coarse sand, think of slicing a piece of sand—a "sand divot"—about the size of a dollar bill when you make contact. You enter the sand on one end of the bill and exit the sand on the other; the ball is where George Washington's picture is on a greenback. On white, fluffy sand, hit the sand well behind the ball so that the club stays under the ball for a longer time before coming up and out.

The Rules of Golf for Sand Bunkers

Players at all levels take needless penalties when they find themselves in the sand because they do not know the rules. The rules below seem to be the ones that are continually broken in the normal course of play, by Sunday golfers to touring professionals.

- You cannot touch the sand with your club or your hand to test the sand. If you make a practice swing make sure that you do not hit the sand with your club.
- You cannot remove stones, twigs, leaves, animals, or anything else that is part of nature from the bunker. (Some courses have a local rule that will allow you, for safety, to remove a stone near your ball, but this must be posted.) You may remove man-made items such as cigarette or cigar butts, candy wrappers, or other trash.
- There is no penalty if you hit someone else's ball from the bunker. You must go back and find your own ball and play it. If the ball is plugged in the sand you may gently remove the sand and move the ball to identify it. You must replace it and the sand before playing it.
- If you have to take an unplayable lie in a bunker, you must drop the ball in the bunker and not place it on top of the sand.

Playing from Firm Sand

On some courses, the sand seems to be packed down so that the overall texture is more like loose dirt than real sand. This is one case where bounce may work against you. The problem is that instead of digging into the ground, the sand wedge might bounce off the top and into the ball, sending it screaming over the green. This occurs fairly often. With firm sand, I like to use my pitching wedge, as it has a lot less bounce than the sand wedge, and digs into the ground and skims the ball out nicely. This is a tricky shot, so practice it whenever you can.

Playing a Bunker with a High Lip

If you must get the ball up quickly because there is a steep lip in front of you, try to lower your body a little by bending your knees a little more than usual to "sit down." Open your club face wide and widen your stance. Let the club come under the ball in a sliding move so that you slice the sand with a club face that is almost flat to the sand. The ball will pop up and out and have a good deal of spin on it as well.

Plugged Lie

If a ball falls into a bunker from a high shot it might just plug into the sand. Your normal bunker shot will not work because you cannot dig deep enough to get under the ball and slide the club forward. In this situation you have two good options: You can square your club face to the ball and swing down and through the ball with a strong motion. This is sometimes called snowplowing. The only problem is that the ball will come out low and run a great deal. The good news is that it is out of the bunker. The other option is to open your club face, bring the club almost straight up, and then slam it down right behind the ball. The sand will displace in a way that the ball pops out relatively softly and will only roll a moderate distance once it comes out.

You need to practice this shot in order to build trust in yourself. Toby Lyons would throw several balls into a trap and step on them and have me make that chopping motion of slamming the club down behind the ball to get it out. The move seems to go against every golfing sense you have developed, but it works. When you try this shot, you will find yourself laughing as the ball pops up and out after you swing the club like you are chopping wood. I am glad I learned that shot from Toby, as it comes in handy more often than you would expect.

The Fried Egg

The shot called the fried egg occurs on courses that have soft sand. Your ball lands and displaces sand so that it sits in the middle of a crater. The best way to play this shot is similar to a plugged lie. Square the club face and strike the sand just behind the back of the crater with a steep descending blow and make a short follow-through. The club will move the crater and ball all in one move. The ball will fly into the air but will not have much spin on it, so don't worry if it rolls. You might not be able to get a fried egg shot close to the pin, but your objective is to get the ball out of the bunker and onto the green. If you think in this manner, you are thinking about scoring well. Too often, golfers try to get more than they should out of plugged or fried-egg lies by trying to spin them out close to the pin. The usual result is to leave the ball in the bunker and to make a big number when one could have been avoided by some calm calculation.

Uphill and Downhill Lies

Every so often your ball will come to rest on a slope in a bunker. The average golfer flubs this shot because he or she sets up poorly and is afraid of what can happen from previous experiences. You just need a little know-how and some confidence to play these shots.

For an uphill lie in the sand, let your shoulders match the slope of the hill as you set up. Set your weight on your right, or back, foot for good balance. The key to the shot is to come into the ball at a shallow angle so that you take a small slice of sand from under the ball to get it up and out. Two ways to mess up this shot are to slam the club into the sand behind the ball and drive the ball farther into the sand itself, or to try to pick it off the sand, which will send the ball flying over the green.

On a downhill slope, set your weight on your front foot for balance and make a very upright swing to come down and slide the club under the ball.

These shots should not produce any anxiety once you have practiced them and know how to play them. Average golfers probably get sick of pros telling them that sand shots are easy, as they provoke such fear in the higher-handicap player. The successful sand shot is grounded in a positive mental approach, is honed in practice to build confidence and self-esteem, and is executed without stress or anxiety. Tension—not the sand—is your enemy in a sand shot. Relax, breathe, and feel smooth as you play out of a bunker.

Practice Routine for Sand Shots

You can make excellent progress and become a great bunker player with a good practice routine and good mechanics, as described above. Developing an ability to play bunkers can take you off the rolls of average players and onto that of good players because successful bunker shots can subtract a significant number of strokes from your average score. I have seen many relatively good players who are terrible at getting out of the bunker and just resign themselves to a double or triple bogey once they land in the sand. This is a silly and defeatist attitude that is a waste of ability. Learn the principles of a bunker shot and take a lesson if necessary. I learned to gain confidence from having Toby Lyons drill me over and over on how to play from the sand. It seemed hard work at the time but once I learned how to play the shots from the sand they were in my repertoire forever, thanks to Toby's guidance. I practice at least ten bunker shots every time I hit balls, just to stay sharp and keep my confidence level up.

Historical Note on Bunkers

You enjoyment may be surprised to find out that bunkers in golf were not the diabolical invention of some golf-course architect. In the early days of the game in England and Scotland, livestock would graze on the land that was too sandy for cultivation. Farmers would place chests, or bunkers, filled with feed into the side of a hill for the animals. As the livestock walked over to feed from the bunkers of grain, they dug out hollows into the sides of the hills. As the land became used for golf courses these hollowed-out places were left in place; later, "bunkers" were created as hazards, to add to the fun and difficulty of the game.

The Game within the Game: Putting

Putting has often been called the game within the game as the stroke, strategy, and ball movement are almost completely different from those of the rest of the game. As I pointed out earlier, the three-inch putt counts the same as the 300-yard drive, much to the chagrin of many great players, such as Ben Hogan. While this may not seem fair in the overall scheme of things, if we put a price on skills, the fact remains that putting makes up almost half of our score. You must first accept this fact and free yourself of thinking that golf is "really" about hitting a long ball or accurate irons. Golf has many facets involved in scoring well, and one of the most important is putting.

Putting can be the skill component that allows you to dramatically better your scores. You are allowed 36 putts in regulation. It is the only time that the golf game allows you actually to miss a shot. The ideal framework for a par round would be to hit every drive in the fairway, hit every approach shot on the green, and then take two putts. The allowance of two putts actually allows you to miss one that you might make. While few of us ever plays that model round, it would be extremely frustrating to hit 18 greens in regulation and make two putts every time to finish with a score of par. This "missed" shot actually allows us to make par when we miss a green and two-putt from long distance to make a par. Even better, it allows us to go under par with a birdie or eagle at times to remove bogeys from our scorecard as if we had an eraser.

If your average score is 85 right now and you take 36 putts on average, you can make dramatic improvement in your scores by learning how to putt. The importance of putting cannot be overemphasized. If you just make one putt go in better than your average once every three holes, your average score will drop to 79. You did not have to drive, hit an iron, pitch, or chip one stroke better. As you begin on a plan to better your putting, remind yourself that you can change your scoring with something that is within your reach and, more important, within your capability. You or I cannot hit a drive or iron as far or straight as Tiger Woods, but we are capable of improving our putting dramatically. We may never putt as well as Tiger, but in this area we can close the gap between our game and his as in no other way.

To become a good putter, you should start with a holistic view of putting. The word itself comes from "putting" the ball into the hole. Putting the ball into the hole is the prime objective of every putt. Putting, like any other way of hitting a golf ball, is a blend of mental acuity and mechanics operating synergistically.

No other area in the game of golf lends itself better to visualization and imagery than putting. The very best putters, such as Brad Faxon, say that they "see" the ball go into the hole. They are able to find a line that looks correct to them and then imagine the ball traveling to the hole and dropping into the cup. They hear the sound and sense the feeling of accomplishment before they ever stroke the ball for real. This mental approach works, and it is essential to every player who wants to become a good or great putter. Let your mind take over and your body go along for the ride. That silky, smooth stroke that we see from the best putters in the world does not come from a drill or "muscle memory." Muscles do not have memories. Our minds sense and respond to a feeling associated with imagery that has been entered in the mind and the information is relayed to our muscles.

The best putters are in a state of heightened awareness. They feel what their arms and shoulders should do in response to the putt, which they have already experienced in their minds. They feel balanced on their feet with no tension and a mind free of doubt or mechanical thoughts. You will know that you are approaching that heightened sense of awareness when you hit a good putt, or a poor one, and know it immediately. In addition, you will know what went wrong on a bad putt because your feeling for the smooth stroke will tell where the error occurred. When this occurs, you have made a breakthrough in advancing your game.

Some of my students in golf have complained that they can putt well on the putting green but simply cannot make putts under pressure. I usually ask them where the pressure is coming from and why it is present in their minds. Pressure in golf comes from within. We must remember that we control our own emotions. We allow fear, worry, doubt, anxiety, frustration, and self-defeatism to take up mental space. Of course we are aware of persons, places, and outside circumstances, but we have the power to control the amount and type of stimulation that we allow to sway our minds.

If you choose to let positive and enriching thoughts serve as your personal motivators, the chances of success are increased exponentially. If, on the other hand, you play with feelings that you must win or that you are not a worthwhile person or are a failure, you are creating a sense of pressure that is based on negative emotions. You must make the choice to accept yourself as being worthy of playing well. Know that the practice and devotion that you have put in to practice has allowed you to perform at a level better than ever before. Accept the change without pressure. Let the good things that happen in golf reinforce your spirit and the mistakes serve as prompts to remind you of areas in which you have more to learn.

There have been players who have made the PGA Tour and LPGA Tour with phenomenal ball-striking skills, only to fail to stay at the top because they could not putt at the level of competence required to play among the best. This is the main reason why there are always fresh faces seeking a Tour card but few who make it. I have played with brilliant surgeons who have eye-hand coordination far beyond 95 percent of the population but they cannot roll a ball three feet in a straight line because they lack the mechanics and knowledge of the putting game to succeed. Then there is a paradoxical phenomenon that seems to be represented by at least one player at every club: he or she scrapes the ball from tee to green and then seems to make every putt and usually ends up scoring somewhere in the high 70s.

You could take the majority of players from the Nationwide Tour or the top 150 PGA club professionals and if you could zap them with the putting proficiency of taking about 27 putts per round, they would suddenly be in the top 150 on the PGA Tour. In golf nothing separates the bad from the good and the good from the great players as clearly as putting.

The last type of player is one that we have all seen or played against—one who made us wonder what happened after we lost a match. I used to play with one player who hit a low slice off of the tee, then a line drive that bounced and rolled somewhere near the green. He would then chip or pitch his ball onto the green, but not particularly well, and proceed to make the putt for par. It seemed as if he was struggling to break 100 as he swung awkwardly and hit terrible golf shots that spent most of the time bouncing down the fairway. But the awkward swings and ugly shots were mitigated by the smooth, silky stroke that rolled the ball into the center of the cup almost automatically. The triple-figure score that his swing seemed to be producing was actually in the 70s most of the time and he ranged in the seven-to-eight handicap range. I do not know if I would enjoy playing golf that way, as hitting good drives and iron shots are part of the fun of golf, but his game opened my eyes to the importance of putting. How could someone look so bad but score so well? My answer is that this man is a good golfer. Putting is part of the game of golf and he excels at the one part that enables him to be a single-digit player. If his scores are consistently better than those of the 10 to 15 handicappers at the club, it means that he is a better player because he scores lower. When you turn in a scorecard, they do not analyze how that score was made.

When a player at the 19th hole says that he shot an 80 but couldn't make a putt to save his life, he is saying that he can play some of this game pretty well but other parts not too well; that he should have had 73 if he had just made a few putts. What about the 20 handicapper who says he could have scored 73 if he had hit his drives 250 yards down the middle every time. It is the same. Putting is not an afterthought. A good golfer is always a good putter, and great golfers are always great putters.

I firmly believe that putting is grounded in the mental aspect of performance. Of the three realms of learning—cognitive, affective, and psychomotor—I believe that the affective realm is the key to improvement in putting.

Let's look at how affective traits have helped make great athletes great. First, they loved their sport. They loved their sport so much that they would practice and work at it far beyond what other kids would do when they were young. There was a joy in practicing and a joy at succeeding. It was never work.

Years ago, I refereed the first basketball game that Patrick Ewing ever played. He was about eleven years old, six foot three, and painfully thin. He ran, dribbled, and shot awkwardly. Smaller players stole the ball out of his hands and drove past him with a little head fake. I remember the other team making fun of him for being so tall yet so awkward and totally lacking in any semblance of being a basketball player. Patrick fell in love with basketball and began to practice every day of the year. In bitter cold, he would shovel the snow from an outdoor court on a public playground in Cambridge, Massachusetts. He would play by himself and rehearse moves that he saw on television until they became his own. He never stopped practicing and making himself better, because he loved what he was doing. In high school he had my friend Mike Jarvis as his coach. Over four years Mike brought him along, gradually introducing the finer points of the game until Ewing headed for Georgetown as a national force in college basketball.

You need not have total devotion like Ewing nor give as much time as he did to become a great putter. But you do need to start with what the 11-year-old Ewing had: a love of the game. Learn to love to putt and become great at putting. Take joy from becoming very good at rolling the ball into the hole. Use your quiet pride to help build the self-esteem that is needed to separate yourself from the pack.

Earlier, I said that I believed that putting was a product of our affective learning process. If we come to believe that we are good putters, we will become good putters. The top players in all sports have streaks: a baseball player hits .450 for the month of July; a basketball player makes seven three-point shots in a row; Tiger Woods plays the treacherous greens at Augusta under pressure and does not have one three-putt in 72 holes. Sure, their skills are honed through practice and tremendous concentration and focus, but the one ingredient that produces streaks both good and bad is mental attitude. In my academic field, all of our studies are based on research that has to be valid—generating results that support the hypotheses that are repeatable. The streaks mentioned above were not caused by what those players had for breakfast, their biorhythms, or sudden hormonal shifts that came and disappeared mysteriously. Streaks, both good and bad, are caused by the players' feeling of confidence and self-esteem—or lack of it—at the time of the streak. The player who hit .450 for July will say to reporters that the ball looked big to him; the basketball player will say that it just felt right. The ball was still the same size and the basketball felt the same as every other one that the player shot. The difference is that the success they felt early caused their minds to tell them that they could repeat the action over and over if they wanted to do so.

I watched Larry Bird win a three-point shooting contest once at the NBA All-Star game. He was launching the ball into the air toward the basket and was reaching for the next ball a fraction of a second after the first had left his hand. The balls fell into the net without touching the rim time after time. I was amazed at Larry's skills, but I also wondered what his mind-set had to be in order for him to perform so reliably with such a remarkable degree of accuracy. He threw the shots up as if they were already programmed in his mind and all he had to do was launch the ball up and move on, knowing the ball would hit nothing but net. His mind was firing in complete harmony with his body because he trusted his body to just do what it was supposed to do. He realized his ability at being the best in the world at that moment and just went with it.

Streaks are periods when our belief system has been altered concerning how we perceive ourselves. Past experience may tell us that we can make a putt, but what if our mind gives us a self-perception that we are one of the ten greatest putters in the world. You might say, well I have evidence that would shoot that theory down. I am offering you a positive framework that will transform you into a good or great putter without any tricks or gimmicks. Forget the evidence that you are a poor putter. You were putting with a mind of a guy who was a good hitter but hit .210 for the month of July. The ball looked small and I just didn't feel right at the plate. That mind-set is not the one that we are going to use to evaluate you as a putter. From this day forward, you are one of the world's top ten putters every time you step on a green. The positive framework can be built on past successes, like Larry Bird's ability to shoot three-pointers with complete confidence.

Earlier I asked you to remember your all-time career round on your home course. Mine was 46. I want you to go through the 18 holes of your course and remember a great putt that you made on each hole, be it for a birdie, par, or even an eagle. You should finish with 18 putts, all of which bring a little smile of accomplishment and pride. Allow your mind to let go and trust it to make you a great putter. It was not someone else making those putts, nor was it what you had for breakfast. It was your mind telling you that you can make the putt. Putting is a process-oriented, not a result-oriented, entity. Your focus should be on mastering the process and building confidence in your ability. The results will appear like a bonus in your paycheck.

Have you ever been behind a putt looking down the line when you just had an overwhelming feeling that you were going to make that putt? Chances are that most of the times you had that the feeling, you made the putt. Often after a long putt, players will say they knew they were going to make it. They just had a feeling. This is the power of the mind in action. The self-esteem, self-concept, attitude all came together to produce a feeling of solid confidence. There was no doubt, hesitation, or wayward thoughts. They were in the zone for that moment and they were like Larry Bird launching a three-pointer. Our goal is to create a routine and a mind-set combined with practical mechanics and knowledge to allow you to bring up these moments of freedom and confidence at will.

What separates poor putters from really good ones is a combination of the proper mental framework and sound mechanics. I feel that the mental framework is far more important as I have seen great putters with rather awkward mechanics but I have never known a good putter who has a poor mental approach to putting. The thing that brings both elements together is a good routine. Doing the same thing over and over for each putt will allow you to check yourself to make sure that you are clearing your mind to be free, are filled with confidence, and know what to do with the putt in front of you.

As a Marine, I was taught to fire a rifle by expert marksmen. The Marine Corps puts a premium on every Marine's becoming very proficient with his weapon. One of the pre-shot routines was called BRASS: *B* for "breathe"; *R* for "relax"; *A* for "aim"; *S* for "sight"; and *S* for "stroke." I found that this routine lends itself very well to putting. The letters stand for the immediate things that you should do before firing a round with your rifle, or your putter.

B—breathe. Holding your breath or breathing irregularly or shallowly creates tension. Breathing helps us to think clearly and have our mind and muscles work together.

R—relax. As you exhale, let all tension or anxiety leave you. Tight muscles will cause a quick and uneven movement as you putt. The club head will go back too quickly. Feel relaxed and comfortable so that your hands are receptive to feel. Letting the club head hover on the top of the grass is a great way to gain this relaxed feeling, as you are getting ready to start the stroke.

A—aim. Check the aim of your putter face and the interim spot that you have picked out along your intended line. Make sure you are pointed to where you want the ball to roll.

S—sight. Look at the hole while you are over the ball. Drag your eyes back and hold the picture of the hole in your mind's eye. You will putt with this picture in your mind.

S—stroke. Make a confident stroke, knowing that you have done everything possible to make the ball go into the hole. Stroke the ball with the expectation of having it drop.

BRASS is actually a routine within a routine, one I use just before and as I stroke the ball. It is just one of many routines that serve to help us become consistent by making sure that we have taken a series of positive steps to ready ourselves before every putt (or other golf stroke). Putting is hard enough as it is but you can become a good or even great putter by developing the routine, the mental awareness, and the sound mechanics needed.

Reading the Greens with Your Eyes

All great putters are able to read the greens so that they know how much a ball will break in a certain direction. Reading a green does not start only when you crouch down behind your ball. Good putters drink in the total picture of a green as they approach it. As you walk toward a green, look near and far for high features of the terrain such as small hills or mounds near the green or mountains in the distance. Try to imagine a strong downpour of rain and visualize how water would drain off the green. Look for low points near the green and the direction to any body of water , whether a pond, a stream, or an ocean. See if there are any danger areas that would cause your ball to veer off course and send it far off line. The draining features and deceptive slopes are architectural designs that are part of every green. As you look at the big picture, let your mind be uncluttered to gather the information.

Once on the green, mark your ball and clean off any dirt or mud. While your fellow playing partners are getting to the green look at the grass. If the grass is shiny, the grain is with you and the ball will roll smooth and fast. If the grass is a dark green, the grain is against you and the ball will roll slower and may even bounce along the top of the grass. From your initial big picture look at the green, note how the high terrain features will cause the ball to move away from them. Putts tend to break away from the mountains and toward the water.

Reading the Greens with Your Feet

We learn through our senses. In the first part of reading the greens we placed an emphasis on the visual aspect of gaining information. The next sensory input that we can use is feeling. We are not allowed to touch the green with our hands to test the texture of the turf, but we have to walk on the green, so our feet become our sensors. From the side of your line, walk half way to the hole. Feel how soft the turf below your feet feels. If it is soft and lush, the putt will tend to roll slower than usual but will be true. If the ground is hard or sand, look for the putt to be quick and have a lot of break to it. At the halfway point, and from the side toward which the ball will break, examine the entire line of the putt. See how much break there appears to be and pick a spot where you think the ball will lose its speed and break the most. That point will become your target; you sight on a breaking putt and not the hole. Continue to walk your line and feel the slope of the green to determine whether there are any subtle rises or drops in the green that you can not detect with your eyes.

Look at the area behind the hole. If you miss a little long, will the ball stop near the hole or run away? Will you be left with an easy comeback putt?

Some players like to get behind the hole and look back to the ball. I personally do not like this as I feel this gives a contrarian perspective that confuses our minds. Get behind your ball and either crouch or bend down to see the how the green flows along your line. You are now gradually narrowing your focus, from the big picture to walking for feeling to determining the path of the ball.

I cannot emphasize too much that you need to get out of your way here and not become overanalytical. Players who agonize over reading a putt appear to be in doubt and only compound their anxiety by taking longer and longer to read the putt. I get flustered when I see a 25 handicap take an extraordinarily long time reading his putt only to miss it by ten feet. Then onto the next green where he goes through the same thing again; as if his game were refined to the point where a subtle read of the line will ensure that he makes the putt. I think television has hurt the game in this instance, as many beginners feel they have to look like PGA professionals at the Masters as they go through their pre-putting routine.

Our eyes and our minds are the best instruments that we have for reading putts. They will not deceive us and will not lie to us. Here is a principle to live by on the greens: *your first read is most likely the best and most accurate one!* Your mind has been gathering data, and when you look down the line of your putt, your mind can figure out the amount of break and the force needed to get the ball into the hole without any outside or conscious input from you. It is the came principle that allows an outfielder in baseball to catch a fly ball. He sees the ball in the air as it comes of the hitter's bat, he runs at a pace that will bring him under the ball based on what his brain feeds him as to how much the ball will travel and where it will come down. If you asked that same player to do the parabolic equation to determine the flight character-istics of the ball and to determine the speed that he needs to run to get under it in time, he would never be able to do it. Our brains know how to do these things very well as they have been developed for thou-sands of years as part of our survival skills. Thus, when you look at a putt from behind the ball, trust your brain to give you the correct read. Past experience on the green, input from watching others, and input from a partner may add additional helpful data. You need to decide what data to accept and what to ignore. The main point is not to think and dwell too much as this will only cause negative emotions to flow.

From behind the ball, determine whether there is a break in the putt. The break will be more pronounced as the ball slows down, so a slope near your ball will not have nearly the effect as one near the hole. Select the point that you want to hit as the peak of the putt. See if you can find an old ball mark, piece of dirt, or old cup to serve as an aiming point. In your mind, draw a white line from that point back to your ball. Pick a spot along the imaginary line about one foot in front of your ball to serve as an interim target. You will roll your ball over that target.

Walk slowly toward your ball and look only at the hole or your target as you approach your ball. Looking at the ball at this stage does nothing to help you make the putt. Looking at the target gives you distance and feel for the putt as your eyes gather in everything on your line and target. Set up and take a few rehearsal strokes while looking at your target. The strokes should have the amount of speed that you will actually make as you putt, based on the input that you are getting from your eyes. Set up to the ball, sight down the line to your target, and draw your eyes back to the ball. Aim at your one-foot target spot and make your stroke to send the ball over the spot at the speed that you have predetermined. Feel free and confident as you stroke the ball.

The feeling of freedom is a key component; free yourself of anything that could intrude and that could cause tension or doubt. Your thought should be to strike the ball solidly and send it on its path to the hole.

Poor putters think completely differently from good putters. The poor putter is saying, "Don't three-putt" to himself while the good putter is saying, "This is going to drop right into the middle." The poor putter is tense and doubtful and hopes the putt will finish near the hole. The good putter is calm, relaxed, and confident that the ball will go into the hole every time. Of course, no one will sink the putt every time. In the 1960s, British scientists used putting machines to hit putts at the perfect speed and perfect line every time. Even the machines could only make eight out of ten putts from ten feet, as tiny variables in the turf sent a few putts off line. The point is that the good putter's level of confidence and freedom from self-doubt allow him to make a stroke that is based on the data that his brain has received and the feeling that he is indeed capable and worthy of making the putt.

When you make the stroke, your only conscious thought is to make solid contact and to roll the ball over that one-foot spot. You can make one-foot putts any time you want to, so if you break your putts down to rolling a one-foot putt at different speeds, you cannot go too far wrong.

With a permanent marker I make little slashes next to the logo of my ball to create a straight line. When I place my ball on the green, I line up this line to my one-foot target as an additional aid. This is perfectly legal and was used by one of the greatest putters of all time, Bob Charles. Once I have gone through my BRASS routine and am ready to stroke the ball, I look at the back of the ball where the putter will make impact. My eyes never leave that spot until the ball is gone. This is what is meant by concentration. You pump up your mind for these brief moments of intense focus that allow you to rise to a new level of proficiency. Poor putters lack this concentration and let their minds and eyes wander. Common errors are watching the putter head go back and forth or following the ball as soon as it has been hit by swiveling the head. Hold your focus on the back of the ball and never look at the putt at all during the stroke. Once you make contact with the ball, keep your head still and let the ball roll out of your view while you look at the grass that was under it.

I have noticed that Tiger Woods strokes a putt and then blinks his eyes before looking up to see where the ball is rolling. This ensures that he has not swiveled or lifted his head during the stroke. More putts are missed because they are not hit properly than because they were misread. Golfers who look up to watch the ball will cause the putter head to make poor contact with the ball. I have taken keeping a steady head to an extreme and have seen touring professionals use the same techniques. It is the best thing that I have ever done for my putting.

When I set up over the ball I know my line and one-foot target. I know the speed that I must hit the ball. There is nothing else I can do to make the putt except to hit it solidly. With this in mind, I stroke the ball and never look up until I hear the ball drop into the cup or my playing partners say something. This prevents me from moving my head so I will always make great contact with the putt. It is such a great feeling to hear the sound of a ball dropping into the cup. Watching the putt travel to the hole does not help in any way. Try this in practice and you will amaze yourself at how many putts drop. Just this little change will bring about a quantum leap in the contact you will make with the ball.

The Mechanics of Good Putting

Sound putting mechanics arise from a consistent commitment to practice. Your goal is to have solid mechanics so that you do not have to think about them on the course. When playing, you need to concentrate only on reading the line, aiming, and striking the ball with confidence. You cannot be thinking of your grip, feet, or posture as you try to make a putt. Your brain would be on overload and would not allow you the freedom to strike the ball to the hole. Learn good mechanics to the point that they are incorporated into your natural way of putting.

The Stance

You should set up to the ball with your shoulders aligned to the target so your arms and hands can flow along your intended line when you make a stroke. Set your putter behind the ball so that it points directly toward your interim target. Then step into your setup and align your shoulders to match the direction of your putter face. There are no other absolutes on lining yourself up to putt.

Place your feet so that you are comfortable and are prevented from moving your legs or body. Your feet should provide balance and stability. In his prime, Arnold Palmer used to putt with a pigeon-toed stance in order to stabilize his legs. Bend from your hips so that your head is directly over the ball or just inside it. This will allow you to swing the putter along your intended line guided by your eyes.

Bend over only as much as is necessary for you to set your putter behind the ball comfortably with your arms hanging down from your shoulders. Find a stance that does not cause any tension in your back or legs and in which you feel comfortable and confident. Aside from the position of your shoulders and head, your stance is pretty much determined by comfort and confidence.

Once over the ball, swivel your head to look at the hole; do not bob up and down to look at it. If you move up and down, you will throw your alignment off after establishing it at the beginning.

The Stroke

You should position the ball slightly forward in your stance so that you strike the ball with a level or a slightly ascending blow. Putters have about 4 degrees of loft so you must place your hands a fraction ahead of the ball at address in order to strike the ball with a flat face. Most good putters take the club back low to the ground. You may stroke the ball and have your putter stay low through contact or come up a little after impact, depending on what is more suitable to you. The key is to make sure that your putter face is facing the target squarely after impact, as you hold it there while the ball is traveling to the hole. If the face is turned closed or opened to the right, you have made an error in your stroke. Always think "Straight back and straight through," as if you were a machine rolling a ball. Every stroke should be made with an accelerating move through the ball. Too often, golfers will make a long backswing and then their brains tell them to slow down so they decelerate through the ball and the putt will go off line or stop well short of the hole. It is better to take a short backswing and a long follow through as this does not slow the putter down. Keep the putter moving through impact so that it feel that you are stroking the ball and not hitting at it.

Much like the full swing, a good putting stroke should have a rhythm to it. It should be consistent every time with only the length of the backswing changing to accommodate distances. I like to practice with a little tempo in mind by saying "One, two" as I putt. "One" starts the putter back and "two" starts it through the ball. This little timing aid prevents making the backswing or forward stroke happen too quickly and helps build a flowing feeling in making a smooth swing with the putter. I have seen players actually practice putting using a metronome to help develop a good tempo.

The Grip

There are more putting grips than I have space to discuss here. The key to any putting grip is that the palms face each other, for this is how they work together. If the hands are turned in different directions, they will fight for dominance and the putts go every which way. Grip the putter lightly so that you can feel the contact with the ball, which helps with distance control and allows you to swing your hands and arms naturally. Your thumbs should be on top of the shaft but do not have to be straight down the middle. As you stroke through the ball your wrists and hands should feel as if they are a unit. The wrists should not bend or break back and forth but should make a small release as the putter moves through impact. Some old instruction books had the hands and wrists holding the putter shaft in a vice-like position that never moved. Good putters always grip lightly and trust the putter to swing and make a slight release toward the hole during the stroke. On long putts you may have to break your wrists a little and bring the club in a mini-golf swing in order to hit the ball a long distance.

A good grip that is neutral will prevent many other problems from creeping into your putting stroke. A good grip will prevent one hand, such as the right, from turning over at impact and pulling the putt to the left of the hole. The neutral grip keeps the wrists, elbows, and arms all in check so they cannot do anything to disturb the stroke.

In the conventional putting grip used by most professionals, the right hand is low and holds the putter where the palm meets the fingers. The left hand is placed on the club so that the last three fingers hold the club while the forefinger overlaps the fingers of the right hand. This grip limits the bending of the left wrist. More and more players are trying a "cross-handed" grip that has the left hand on the bottom and the right hand on top. Jim Furyk has putted this way all his life and is one of the best putters on the Tour. Both Arnold Palmer and Jack Nicklaus have said that if they were starting their careers over, they would begin with the left-hand-low grip for putting. The advantage of this grip is that it prevents the left shoulder from pulling out during the stroke and helps keep the head and shoulders pointing along the line. It gives the putter a good motion, as the wrists cannot make any abrupt motions that will turn the club face off line. Even if you do not use it on the course, you should practice with it at times to feel how your shoulders stay square at impact.

The Roll

All great putters cause the ball to roll true. A true roll has the ball moving in a way that it stays on line and hunts the hole. You should stroke the ball so that it does not bounce and rolls over and over on one circumference. To check to see if you have a true roll and to help you develop one, use a practice ball that has a solid stripe around it.

Place the ball so that the stripe is parallel to your putter face, stroke the ball, and see what happens to the stripe. If the top of the stripe goes forward you have made a good stroke, if the top heads backward at impact, you are putting backspin on the ball and it will bounce. Correct your hand position so make sure that you are striking the ball level or slightly upward. Now, place the stripe so that it points to the hole. Stroke the ball and see if the stripe remains solid as it rolls. If it does, you have put true roll on the ball. If the stripe appears wobbly, you have not made good contact. Practice with striped balls until the ball rolls with a smooth stripe to the hole.

The key to making a good roll is to make sure that your ball hugs the ground and starts rolling as soon as possible. If a ball bounces or skips with a little backspin, it will not get onto your intended line. Striking the ball in the equator is essential. The solid hit from a level or slightly ascending angle will promote a ball that rolls close to the ground. The ball will seem to go a little farther than the force that you put on the strike. This is why you will see touring pros make a short stroke and have the ball travel a good distance. It is not just the fast greens but the way they roll the ball that gets it tumbling toward the hole.

If you are practice-putting when there is dew on the green, look at the impression left by your ball's trail. If there are skips at the beginning, you are making the ball bounce off your putter. While the dew is on the green, practice so that there are few or no gaps in the trail that your ball leaves in the dew. That way you know that you are rolling the ball.

Practice-putting to Make Dramatic Improvement

If you go to any golf course where there is a core of good golfers, take a look at where they are practicing. The majority of players will be hitting balls on the range while the good golfers gravitate to the putting green. What you are observing is the fact that good golfers know where the scoring happens on the course. They have solid games and if they are going to improve or really make a leap in their game, it will come from becoming a better putter.

In a rather backdoor way, good putting makes you an all-around better golfer, for several reasons. For one thing, you can become more aggressive and go after pins on your approach shots. If you miss the green, you can fall back on your strength of getting the ball onto the green and making the putt to save par. If your aggressive approach works, you are looking at a birdie. If you are playing against a player who hits the ball nine miles off the tee, you do not have to feel inferior. You know that you are a better putter and that the playing field is leveled or maybe even tipped in your favor. The average player will make a bogey usually by missing a par putt from about ten feet. As a great putter, you will make more and more of these putts and move away from the ranks of the average. In match play, it is demoralizing to an opponent to see someone roll one putt after another into the hole. Psychologically, the opponent knows that he will have to play above and beyond his capabilities in order to match up against a good putter. Once that happens, the match is yours. I like to think of these putting advantages as residual benefits. They not only lower your score but make so many other things better in your golf game.

Drills and Games for Developing Your Putting

In putting developing a sense of distance is very important. Judging distance is a matter of acquiring good depth perception and translating it to the force of the stroke needed on a particular putt. This leads to concept of touch. You need to build connections in your mind between the force your hands exert on the putter and the distance the ball travels. You can work on depth-perception development, as it is a visual skill that responds to practice and drill. Some people say that you can't teach touch, but you certainly can learn it.

Putting Practice on a Green

Here are some drills that are designed to help you acquire good depth perception in judging distance on a green and linking distance and touch.

Partner putting. Have a friend go with you to the practice putting green. Stand about 40 feet apart and use just one ball. Stroke the ball so that it comes to rest at your partner's feet. He or she will then putt back to you and try to stop the ball at your feet. You can make a competition out of this to see who stops the ball the closest on the most putts. This drill is fun and, more important, forces you to concentrate on distance more than on target. You will be surprised at how quickly you will start to get a better feel from this kind of practice as your mind and depth perception start to coordinate. Change distances after a while and hit putts that have some break in them as well. The more you do this drill, the greater your confidence on the course.

Putt to the edge. Use about three balls to putt 20 to 25 feet. Your goal is to stroke the ball so that it comes to rest just an inch shy of the edge of the green. This removes the pressure of having to hit a target and places your focus on making a stroke to match a distance. This is also a good drill to use when you come to a new course. as it will help you gain a feel for the speed of the greens.

If you can master this drill by stroking three balls very close to the edge of the fringe without going onto it, you are building touch into your mind-body relationship. You are executing what your eyes tell you to do. This skill will allow you to hit those long putts close or into the hole at a greater percentage than you ever dreamed possible, and three-putt greens will start to disappear from your game as well. Three-putt greens are caused mostly by poor distance control. You seldom will miss a putt 10 feet left or right of the hole, but often you will three-putt by hitting the ball 10 feet past or 10 feet short. Once you master distance, the three-putt dilemma ceases to be a worry for you.

Putt to different distances. A good distance drill to make your mind react properly is to set out a little practice area on the putting green. Place tees in the ground at distances and angles all over the green. Putt one ball to a 10-foot target and then carefully line up and putt to a 30-foot target. On this drill, never putt to the same target twice in a row; this will force your depth perception and reading skills to react to a new set of variables each time. Do not rush through this drill by firing putts one after the other. Make each putt as if you were playing in competition. Go through your BRASS routine each time. You are not only learning distance but also perfecting your routine so that it becomes built in, giving you greater consistency and awareness.

Sloppy practice or putting the ball without purpose or careful thought is counterproductive. You not only fail to improve but also tend to build poor habits that will come back to haunt you on the course. The football coach Bill Parcells will tell his team to get off the practice field altogether when he sees his players getting sloppy or just going through the motions. He does this not only to display his displeasure with the team's effort but also because he knows that practicing in this manner will lead to mistakes and injuries once the real games begin. Make your practice-putting quality time and not an endless and mindless exercise.

Uphill and downhill. Putting uphill and downhill putts on a fast green is a great way to develop touch and distance judgment. These are the putts that cause the average golfer to three-putt and make big numbers. The basic tendency is to hit downhill putts way past the hole and leave uphill putts short. Start by hitting 20-foot downhill putts so that your ball dies or just drops over the edge of the cup. You will want your ball to drop into the cup or fall just a few inches short. A ball that goes by the hole can lead to trouble. Use a short backstroke and short follow-through to strike the ball. Hit the ball in the center of your putter to ensure accuracy. Control the distance by the length of the stroke, not the speed. Some players like to hit fast downhill putts on the toe of the putter as this deadens the ball. It can be effective if you practice this method and keep your left hand firm to the line. You must be aware that hitting the ball on the toe may twist the putter and send the ball off to the right, so when you practice, keep the putter square back and through during the stroke.

Increase the distance on your downhill putts so that you can make your short stroke match up nicely with the varying distance. As mentioned above, do not take the club back in a long backswing and then ease into it. It will not work.

On uphill putts, you can accelerate the putter through the ball to make the ball roll up the hill. Try to go past the hole a few inches every time—not more than six. Practice about 20 putts, and have them come to rest within six inches behind the hole for a short tap in. If you leave one putt short, you must start over until you can make 20 in a row that either go into the hole or just past it. This practice will build your confidence and make you become more aggressive on these putts. On an uphill putt, the back of the cup is higher than the front, and this little back board helps you, because a putt that strikes the hole will tend to hit the back and drop in.

On the Course

Let's jump from the practice green to the course. When it comes to making a putt of any substantial difference, contradictory golf adages abound. We have all heard "Never up, never in," meaning to always have your ball traveling at a speed so that if it does not go in the hole it will go past it. Others say you must "die it in" to be a good putter. Jack Nicklaus always favored "dying the ball in," so that the putt would just make it over the front lip. He was probably the greatest clutch putter in the history of the game, so who is to argue with him? On the other hand, his archrival, Arnold Palmer, would launch putts that struck the hole at a good speed or went by 4 to 6 feet. In his prime he was such a good putter that he knew he would make the comeback putt, so he was not afraid to go after the first one. Tiger Woods seems to be in the middle. He is aggressive on some putts, when he needs to make it, but cautious when a par is a good score.

Once you have learned to control your distance through practice, you can think of using your distance control to score well. A good way to look at putting is to think of the concept that there are only four ways to miss a putt: right, left, long, or short. If you make up your mind never to miss a putt short, you have just eliminated one quarter of the causes that putts are missed for the rest of your life. This does not mean that you will automatically slam every putt across the green like a rocket. It means that you will use good judgment to stroke each putt so that if it misses, it stops about one foot past the hole. By doing this you will accomplish several objectives:

- You will give your ball a chance to go into the hole that a short putt will never have.
- You will stroke your putt at a speed that will hold to your intended line. A ball that loses speed near the hole is more likely to break more and to be influenced by inconsistencies in the texture of the green.
- You will tend to keep the ball on the high side of the hole, which guarantees a chance for the ball to go in as compared to a ball on the low side of the hole. A ball on the high side of the hole is always moving in the direction of your target.
- By stroking the ball with slightly more force you will have a consistent roll and a smoother stroke. A stroke that tries to dictate distance by slowing into the ball will send it well off line.
- You will make more putts and your confidence level will rise.

Practicing for Accuracy

Accuracy in all sports comes from starting small and building out. A young child learning to hit a baseball will start with hitting the ball from a tee and progress from there to soft underhand tosses to slow pitches and gradually to fast balls over a period of years. By starting small and moving to big, the developmental process is built sequentially as skills are acquired. It is the same with putting.

Make the short ones. A good way to build accuracy and confidence is to make three-foot putts over and over. Focus on each putt as if it were important and stroke the three-footer into the cup with authority. Try to have the ball enter the middle of the hole every time. Make 20 putts in a row. If you miss one, you must start over. Listen to the ball drop into the cup; place this sound in your memory and relish it so that you can call it up in your mind as you are getting ready to putt on the course. Expect to hear the sound every time you stroke a ball in practice or on the course. This is a great way to practice just before playing, as making 20 putts in a row along with the sensory stimulation of the ball rattling in the cup places you in a heightened state of confidence.

By hitting accurate three-foot putts, you develop the ability to roll the ball accurately over a target that is close to you. On the course, you will use an interim target about one foot from your ball and along your target line to the hole. If you can make a one-foot putt with accuracy, you can roll your ball along your intended line every time you putt on the course. In addition, should you miss a putt from a distance, you will be very confident in making the comeback three-foot putt because it has been mastered in practice. On the very short putts, stay still and listen for the ball to drop. Pick a spot to roll the ball just a foot in front of you and stroke the ball so that it goes on a straight line to the hole. You do not have time to look up and watch a three-foot putt, so do not try to guide it in with your eyes. Whenever you see a player miss a very short putt, whether a beginner or touring pro, it is usually caused by the player's looking up to see the ball roll to the cup. The result is a weak stroke that causes a poor roll or a putt that is pulled left of the hole. When we miss a short putt the cause is usually a mental error, not a mechanical one. Take your time, align your putter and your shoulders, and stroke the ball so that your putter head "chases" the ball to the hole while your head stays still. Stroke these short putts firmly because the area around the cup is usually rough from players stepping near it and all the activity involved in tending a pin and tapping in and retrieving balls from the cup. If you stroke the ball firmly, it will roll over these rough spots and find the hole more often. In addition, on softer greens, the activity near the hole will tend to press the ground down, leaving the hole and cup slightly elevated. A soft putt will veer off this crown whereas a firm one will ride into the cup.

Putt to a tee. A small target such as a tee refines your accuracy skills. Place a tee in the ground and putt to it from five feet. Stroke the ball so that you hit the tee solidly but do not knock it over. This practice forces you to narrow your focus and requires you to place a premium on accuracy with your stroke. If you use this practice drill before you play, the holes on the course will appear larger and your confidence will soar. Being able to manipulate perception is a tried and true method of developing your mind skills to enhance your performance. As a youngster pitching in Babe Ruth leagues and high school, I would finish my warm-ups by throwing fastballs from about 75 feet. My coaches did not like to see me doing this and at the time I found it hard to explain why I did it. But after throwing about ten fastballs from 75 feet, when I walked onto the mound the catcher looked like he was only a few feet away from me. I pitched with a feeling of having great strength and confidence in being able to throw hard over what now looked to me like a "short" distance. After you have hit a tee with your putts from five feet, when you look at the first hole, you will have a surge of confidence in putting that little ball into that great big crater.

Circle the wagons. Place about ten balls in a circle around the hole, each ball about five feet from the hole. One by one, line up each putt and make it as you move around the circle. Chances are you will have to make adjustments for different breaks, so you must read each putt. The circle drill will both hone your reading skills and develop your mind to adjust to different angles that you will face on the course.

Track putting. Place two two-by-fours along on the green about six inches apart, to make a railroad-track effect wide enough for your putter to fit just inside the boards. From six feet, stroke a ball from the middle of the track to the hole. You will be forced to bring your putter straight back and straight through every time. This is a good drill when you find yourself in a putting slump as it makes you stroke the ball squarely each time or you will strike the boards during your stroke.

Eye hooks and string. This is by far my favorite putting drill to build your stroke and increase your confidence. Many touring professionals carry this simple device in their bags to practice wherever they go. Get two six-inch eye-hook screws and about 12 feet of string, and tie the string to each eye hook. Set the screws into the green so that one screw is right behind a hole and the other extends away from the hole. Place about five balls under the string at two-foot intervals, the first ball about two feet from the cup. Place your head over the first ball and stroke it along the string and into the cup. Go to the next ball, place your head over it, and continue on making the putts, letting your putter follow the string. You will be amazed to roll in the putts one after the other with ease. It will seem as if you cannot miss! Do this drill every day for 30 days and your mind will absorb that overwhelming feeling of confidence from making putts from two to 10 feet with precision. When you remove the string, the stroke should still be in your memory bank. Commit to 30 days of practice with this drill and you will become better than you had ever hoped to be.

Putting for Real

As you play the game of golf and come to putt, call upon the immense confidence that you have gained from your disciplined practice. You should have a feeling of freedom, since you are approaching your putt with a routine that will guarantee consistency. You have developed a fine sense of distance, force, and touch and you have acquired remarkable accuracy. Remind yourself of this and talk to yourself about how good you really have become. There is no need to tell others, as they will see the results without your mentioning a word of how you have developed into a good or great putter. You have earned the right to feel very confident, for the work you have put into your practice is the reason you know that you are good on the greens.

When you stand behind the putt, go through your routine, read the putt from knowledge and experience, and trust your stroke to strike the ball solidly so that it hits your spot, tracks the line that you visualized, and drops into the hole. Of course, you will not make every putt but you will be close on every putt. Three-putts will become rare and your scores will reflect your new proficiency.

Carry yourself with confidence and enjoy the feeling of being a very good putter. Think of yourself as being one of the best putters in your club or one of the best putters of anyone that you have ever played. This is not false bravado, but rational expectations derived from the careful practice and diligence that you have brought to your putting game. Let your confidence give you the freedom to allow you to score low.

Putting Strategy

On the course, you know how to read greens and how to feel distance and stroke the ball to have it go in or stop just behind the hole. You now must factor in the round's current situation and the putt in front of you as to what you should do. For one thing, always try and make every putt. Forget about a three-foot ring, inside the leather, or a wash-tub. If you try to make every putt, you will be closer than trying to factor in missing points. Stay with the routine you have developed in practice and trust the stroke that has served you well.

Use as many strategies and techniques as you can to take the advantage in making your putt. The following ideas have worked well to help putters in competition:

- For putts longer than 25 feet, always have someone tend the flag-stick. A standing person offers a better target for depth perception and perspective than only a hole. Artists develop an eye for perspective so that they can draw figures and structures in scale. Someone standing next to your target is a great aid. In addition, you may use the person's feet as your aiming point if there is a break in the putt. For example, you can look at the person's feet and use them as your focus point for the line that you want your ball to start along. Asking the person to place his or her foot in a certain place is against the rule of golf.
- Watch the chips and putts of your playing partners to see how the ball rolls on the green and what kind of breaks occur near the hole. Do not try to gauge distance from watching another's putt because it is difficult to know how hard or solid the ball was struck. Observe how the slope and grain affect the roll of the ball.
- If playing best ball with a partner, one player may go first to make a par so the other has a "free" run at the birdie as an example. However, before the round, talk this strategy over with your partner as some players do not like to make the par putt under pressure or have a "free" go at a birdie. Often, the player with the "free" putt will slam the ball way too hard so that it never has a chance

of going into the hole. He or she wants to make sure that they got the ball past the hole and "gave it a chance," when actually they lost the sense of making the putt. Personally, I like my partners to hold their putt and let me focus on making the birdie with no burden of getting it way past the hole.

• Rest your mind when you are on the green. Avoid becoming the kind of player who gets on the green and goes into a frantic search to determine every possible break or subtle nuance of the green as he circles the hole like a predator around a prey. Relax, breathe, and trust your first read. There is no reason to magnify the intensity of putting by scrutinizing everything on the green. Get behind your ball, get your read, and stay in your routine. Go about your business in an efficient manner so that no tension can build up. Step up to your putt with a feeling of total confidence and put your best stroke on it. You have completed the process the best you can; now let the result happen. You can only control so much. It is interesting to note how more and more touring professionals are getting away from the drudgery of poring over a putt before setting up to the ball. Modern players are learning to trust themselves and their minds to be correct and go about putting at a good pace with a feeling of lightness and freedom in their whole presence on the green. Although a wonderful putter, Jack Nicklaus tended to spend an inordinate amount of time analyzing a putt before putting. Nicklaus's deliberate style was his very own and he was playing for a living and playing at the highest level of the game. Today's professionals are more in tune with modern trends in mind-body relationship. See it—feel it—do it.

• Look for danger. If there are slopes on the green that can cause your ball to veer well off line, be cautious and take two putts to get away from the trap that has been set. Always examine the area behind the hole to see what would happen if you were to go one foot beyond the hole: Would the ball catch a ridge or funnel that would channel it away? Sometimes pin placements seem to be unfairly placed in treacherous positions. When you come to one of these pins, play conservatively and make two putts and walk away with a par. Learn to fight for your birdie on another green.

- Keep your emotions on an even keel. Try to stay in the present. Getting angry or overelated about something that happened on the last hole will not serve you well, as it is now a distracting emotion. You need to approach each putt in the moment. You begin with "tabula rasa"—a blank slate—each time. Make your read, feel your confidence, see the line to the hole, pick your interim target, and roll the ball into the cup. Whatever took place before or might be ahead has no bearing on your present putt unless you bring it into the equation by allowing it into your thinking.

- Think process, not score. Think in terms of doing what you have to do and not of the results. If you stay in tune with your process the results will take care of themselves. A putt can only do two things: it can go in or it can miss. Every golfer in the world misses putts every time he or she plays. It is not life or death if you miss an easy putt. Let it go and move on to the next hole. A friend of mine once said, "There are nine hundred million people in China who do not know or care that I just missed that three-foot putt." If you missed it, it was not from a lack of effort or staying with your process. It is part of the game and it is the part that makes golf so wonderful.

Set a goal for yourself that will allow you to actually attain a higher level of putting performance. As you improve, you need to see that you are actually getting better, and in the last chapter we provide some charts to help you track your game. You can set objectives of making so many three-foot putts in practice in a row and try to keep breaking your personal record. As the personal record of putts made in a row increases, you will know that you are getting better; that feeling of confidence will carry over to your game.

Make a promise to yourself never again to think of yourself as a poor putter. In your self-talk you should no longer belittle yourself after a miss. Carry yourself with a feeling that you have the skills and abilities and the tools of a great putter. This is not wishful thinking. You do have the skills and abilities along with the healthy mental framework within you right now. You have all the tools to be a great putter. Draw on your resources and successes to expand your conscious awareness of how good you really are at putting. Every putt that you hit in practice or on the course will be hit with the stroke of a master and will have a chance of going into the cup. It is all within you and is there for the asking.

CHAPTER SIX

Golf Wellness

GOLF HAS BEEN SLOW TO INCORPORATE ASPECTS OF ATHLETICS THAT ARE taken for granted in other sports. Practice and physical fitness were relatively late in coming to the game. We have all heard the stories of the good-time players who went out partying all night and played great the next day. It was said that Walter Hagen was the consummate playboy who could drink all night. Those who knew Hagen said that he often circulated with a drink in his hand and appeared jovial, but only sipped a little and never really overindulged. I believe that many of these stories are similarly exaggerated—more like folklore than history.

In the late forties and early fifties, Ben Hogan was seen as an anomaly in that he practiced for hours to perfect his swing. Others players at the time simply warmed up or hit shots in practice from time to time. Gary Player was the first PGA star to work extensively on physical fitness and flexibility. Fellow competitors soon took notice when the five-foot-seven, 150-pound player boomed his drives and won majors with regularity.

Tiger Woods's appearance on the scene as a muscular, hardened, and flexible athlete set the standard for others. Players soon realized that they would have to work on their bodies as well as their swings if they were to compete with Tiger. Annika Sorenstam once said, "If the typical PGA Tour player worked out as hard as I do, he'd add thirty yards." Players have now begun to work out in a fitness trailer that follows the tours from site to site.

Good golf depends on mental and physical well-being. If the body cannot perform or the mind cannot function then major improvement and good golf cannot take place. For you to perform at your best, your body needs to be able to respond to the requests that your mind makes of it. To do this, you must look at nutrition, fueling during the pre-round and during the round, building strength and endurance, and, most of all, flexibility. Many people do not think of golfers as athletes, but this is far from the truth.

In recent years, pro golfers have realized the need for a healthy living style, building strength in muscles important to golf, and developing agility to make a smooth swing and prevent injury.

Basic Nutrition

To perform well in golf we do not need to be locked into a stern eating regimen like that of a boxer or weightlifter. We do need to use some common sense and good judgment in our daily eating and drinking habits and give some thought to how we stay fueled on the course. If you are on a program to make dramatic improvement in your game, you must make the commitment to allow your body and mind to function at their optimum. Carbohydrates from good whole food such as cereal, nuts, grains, vegetables, and proteins from lean meat enable our bodies to build and maintain muscle and produce energy needed to perform practice sessions and play rounds without loss of strength and focus. The night before playing, eat a good dinner that will have components of carbohydrates and some protein to fire your muscles and sustain your stamina for the round.

Breakfast on the day of a round should be light yet filling. Cereal, fruit, toast, and a cup of coffee or tea is a standard breakfast that will not overload you or tire you from having to digest things like eggs and bacon. Keep coffee intake to a minimum or go to decaf to avoid the feeling of become anxious or nervous from caffeine. Drink two glasses of water or juice to hydrate your body and aid digestion.

On the Course

The very best players always refuel on the course with fruit, nutrition bars, or a snack to maintain a steady blood-sugar level and to keep the feeling of having energy throughout the round. If you seem to fade over the last few holes, check to see if you have been eating and drinking properly during the round. For some reason golfers more than other athletes neglect this aspect. How often have you seen golfers wolf down a few hot dogs and a beer after nine while making the turn? If you are serious about your game, you must commit to the entire experience of improving, and that includes good nutrition.

Drinking water or a sports drink is essential as dehydration can sneak up on you without your noticing it. I mentioned how the desert can slow your thinking naturally by slowing the mind and body. The lack of fluids will have the same effect. The Israeli Army requires that its soldiers drink eight quarts of water per day during operational phases. You should drink water continuously and set a goal of replenishing yourself with at least two quarts of water during the round, depending on the heat. I try to have a bottle of water filled at all times and drink from it between shots. In golf, the action takes place about 5 percent of the time while the other 95 percent of the time is walking or riding to our ball. Why not use this time productively by keeping our bodies and minds in good shape for the next shot instead of mindlessly traveling around the course? You do not want to be grinding or fretting between shots, so take a break to refresh and renew yourself.

I am not a teetotaler, but alcohol and good golf don't mix. Alcohol has ruined many a round for players of all levels. I have known touring professionals and club players alike who tried to tee it up while hungover. It does not work, for your body is in a recovering mode while it tries to process and eliminate the poisons imbibed the night before. I may have days when I do not play well, but it will never be from being hungover. You need to make a choice. Have fun the night before or have fun the next day on the course. They are usually mutually exclusive.

Building Physical Stamina

Strength and flexibility are essential to playing to your goals. The golf swing is an unnatural movement: we twist around our spines and swing a weighted rod over our heads, toward the ground, and then back over our heads again within about two seconds. Where else in human activity is this type of action considered commonplace? In order to make this unnatural move we must have balance, strength, and flexibility or we will not be able to do the movement efficiently and may even injure ourselves.

In building strength, concentrate on the muscles that are golf-specific. One easy way to ensure that you are working on strengthening your golf muscles is to swing a club—this exercise forces the golf muscles to fire and respond. I like to swing a club designed for exercise called the Swing Fan, which has large plastic fins that provide air resistance as you swing, allowing you to build the specific muscles needed for a powerful swing. Do not swing a club that has a weighted head, as this will make you lose the feel of the club head. Clubs with weighted shafts are fine, as they will help you swing in a proper plane. One word of caution: Avoid swinging weighted clubs or training aids before you play a round. The club will feel different and too light and will throw your natural rhythm and tempo off. I use the strength-building training aids on off days or after I practice.

The best kind of physical preparation for golf, according to experts, is strengthening the internal muscles that support our posture and stretches that allow our muscles to work without tension. It is the freedom of the muscles that creates power and allows us the feel to develop accuracy. I have had several surgeries in the past few years that almost put an end to my playing days. I had wounds from Vietnam that required surgery on my knees and legs that caused pain and stiffness. Dr. Arnold Scheller, the team physician of the Boston Celtics, replaced my knee and then placed me on a year-long recovery plan of physical therapy so I could return to golf. Dr. Chris Olivieri, of Coastal Chiropractic in Cohasset, Massachusetts, has worked with me to both strengthen and stretch my golf muscles to enable me to play well, avoid pain and injury, and achieve the posture I need to perform at my best. Dr. Olivieri gave me a daily routine of stretches and exercises to build golf muscles and the flexibility needed to play my best. I perform these before and after I play, and they have given me a new freedom in my swing, increased my distance, and allowed me to swing with trust that I will not feel pain. Dr. Olivieri's wife, Jennifer, an accomplished athlete, posed for the pictures and provided instructions for the exercises on the following pages.

Exercise 1: Spine Stretch

1. Kneel on the floor on all fours and keep your head up.

2. Tighten your abdominal muscles.

3. Slowly elevate your left arm and right leg until they are straight.

4. Hold for 2 seconds, slowly lower, and repeat on the other side.

5. Perform 3 sets of 10 repetitions.

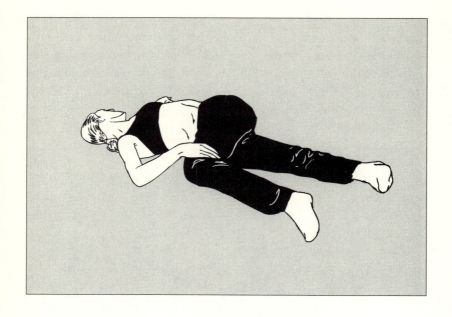

Exercise 2: Hip Stretch

1. Lie on your back and bend your left knee.

2. Keeping your opposite leg straight, pull your left knee up and to the right.

3. Keep your shoulders flat on the floor and look to your left.

4. You should feel a stretch in your lower back.

5. Hold the stretch for 30 seconds and repeat on the other side.

Exercise 3: Quadriceps–Hip Flexor Stretch

1. Lie on your side with your bottom leg stretched out straight.

2. Hold the foot of your top leg and pull your heel toward your glutes.

3. Now thrust your top hip forward.

4. You should feel a stretch in the front of your upper leg.

5. Hold for 30 seconds and repeat on the other side.

Exercise 4: Piriformis–Glute Stretch

1. In a seated position cross your right leg over your left leg.

2. Pull your right knee toward the opposite side of your chest with your left arm.

3. Look over your right shoulder.

4. You should feel a stretch in the right hip and glute.

5. Hold for 30 seconds and repeat on the other side.

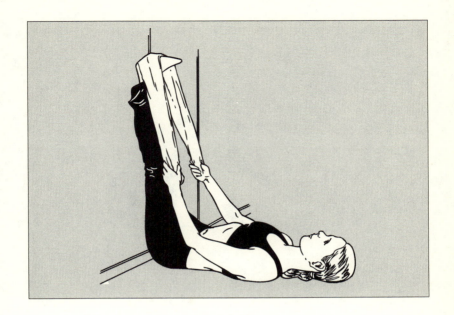

Exercise 5: Hamstring Stretch

1. Lie on your back in an open doorway.

2. Place one leg against the wall and the other leg through the doorway.

3. Keep your back and butt on the floor and the floor leg bent at the knee.

4. Place a towel over the ball of your foot and gently pull it toward you.

5. You should feel a stretch in the back of the upper and lower leg.

6. Hold for 30 seconds and repeat on the other side.

Exercise 6: Lower-Back Stretch

1. Lie on your back with towel roll under neck.

2. Using your arms, pull both knees up to your chest.

3. Hold for 30 seconds.

4. You should feel a stretch in your lower back.

Exercise 7: Chest Stretch

1. Stand in a doorway with your elbows bent at a 90-degree angle.

2. Keeping your back straight and arms against the frame, step through the doorway.

3. Be sure to look straight ahead with your chin slightly elevated.

4. Hold for 30 seconds.

5. You should feel a stretch in your chest.

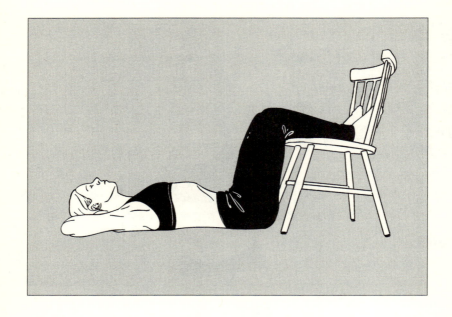

Exercise 8: Abdominal Strengthening

1. Lie on your back on a firm surface.

2. Place your feet on a chair so that your knees are bent at a 90-degree angle.

3. Place your hands behind your head.

4. Tuck your chin and slowly raise your body up until your shoulder blades come off the floor.

5. Hold for 2 seconds and slowly lower back down.

6. Perform 3 sets of 10–20 repetitions.

CHAPTER SEVEN

How Good Do You Want to Be?

How good do you want to be? Now is the time to ask yourself this question, become aware of your answer, and formulate your plan to get where you want to be with your golf game. In a sense, this is where it begins for you. I hope that you have gained the knowledge you need in order to make a good swing or figure out how to play a round of golf and score well. I want you to have a feeling of freedom so that you can get out of your own way by dismissing negative or intrusive thoughts that do nothing but inhibit your game and your journey to improvement. You should be making connections through visualizations and practice to create a greater awareness of the feel of the swing, shot, or stroke that you must make. The cognitive, affective, and psychomotor aspects of learning should meld together to help you make dramatic progress.

When you pose the question to yourself now, assess your skills, abilities, and level of commitment and match them to your goal. There may be many goals depending on these variables, and also time, age, and physical ability. You must have a goal in mind as it is the prize at the end of the journey. It is the purpose behind all that you do. If you do not have a goal, there is no target to shoot at, and you end up firing a rifle into the air or spraying golf balls all over the driving range.

Chances are, you have found elements in your life that have brought you success. It could be in family, academia, business, or a profession. If you think back to the process that brought you to that level of success, most likely there was a goal present at the start. It may not have been formalized in writing but the goal was clear in your mind and determined the path that you had to take to reach it.

When I was in high school, my father asked me what I wanted to do in life. I remember replying that I wanted to be a Marine Corps officer, a doctor, and a golf professional. My answer seemed so grandiose and unrealistic that I felt childish—like a seven-year-old, not a teenager—as the words rolled out of my mouth. My father was a supportive man but tried to caution me to become realistic in my thinking and to give my options more thought. No one in my family had ever gone to college and we lived over a convenience store. My goals sounded more like pipe dreams than targets that would give me purpose in life.

The more I thought of my goals as time passed, the more I came to believe that with incredible determination and blessings, I could attain them. I became a Marine officer and was decorated for action in Vietnam. I continued my studies later to receive two master's degrees and a Ph.D. and went on to a career as a licensed psychotherapist for children. I practiced and worked hard at golf after my children were raised and through school and earned my license as a golf professional. I mention this not out of arrogance but to illustrate that we have the power inside of us to make miracles happen. I believed that as a dreamy teenager and I believe it today and I have lived the dream of setting and accomplishing goals. You have the power and the ability within you to become as good as you can be in golf and in life. I continue to have goals, but they have shifted to such things as helping people by giving golf clinics to inner-city kids and simply making myself a better person in every role that I have in life.

Setting Your Goals

Let's look at a hierarchy of goals that you might have as a golfer:

- Making the PGA or LPGA Tour
- Making it to a professional tour
- Becoming a club professional

- Becoming a scratch player
- Becoming a single-digit-handicapper
- Breaking 80 consistently
- Breaking 90 consistently
- Breaking 100 consistently

Look at these goals and scratch out any that seem unrealistically high or too unambitious. Focus in on one goal listed above and reflect on it. Do you have the skills and abilities needed to work realistically to reach that goal? Are you willing to dedicate the time and effort necessary to reach that goal? Do you truly love the game of golf to the degree that will motivate you to keep working toward your goal? Do you have the capacity and willingness to become a voracious learner who continually seeks improvement through knowledge, attitude, and mind-body exercise?

The questions above should be viewed not as roadblocks but as guideposts. To set out in pursuit of a goal without the values, principles, attitudes, and commitment noted would be to waste your time and effort and set yourself up for frustration. Check yourself to make sure that your goal is a good fit. If you feel confident that your goal is indeed within your reach, go for it. You will never have to ask yourself what might have been if you truly make the effort to achieve your goal. If you set out on the process but never quite make the goal that you set, you will not have failed. The success can be in the process to which you devote time and energy to become better. The worst thing that can happen if you set a goal and follow the guidelines is that you become a much better golfer than you ever expected to be. It is a win-win situation—you cannot really fail as long as you give it an honest try.

One of the best ways to set goals is to visualize what it will be like once you have attained your goal. This is a wonderful technique for planning and analysis in all aspects of your life. It is a way of thinking that places you within the desired environment before it occurs so that you can feel the experience before living it. A young man recently called me to ask some questions about becoming a professional golfer. I explained to him what it entailed and he seemed to know and accept the details of the professional's work. When I asked him if he was ready to give up his amateur status, he hesitated. He had to work that through, as he had not visualized life as a professional: he would never again play in a member-guest tournament, most charity tournaments, or amateur events once he received his card. He decided to keep his amateur status.

Whatever goal you choose in golf, visualize the positive—and negative—consequences for you in your golfing life. Is it becoming a single-digit handicapper? You must know that you will be practicing more often than the average golfer for a greater amount of time. You will need to take lessons on a regular basis and your tournaments will be more oriented toward your gross score than your net performance. You may not want to play with your regular foursome or they may not want to play with you as the gap in performance levels will throw off the usual setup that your playing partners have become used to with you. These are just some of the things that you will notice and become aware of as you visualize yourself as a five handicap instead of a 15. It will change many things in your golf life, so be aware of the changes on the horizon. We have spoken earlier of the difficulties that change can bring.

Once you have determined a realistic goal for you, one that will fit you well in life, set your plan in motion. The preceding chapters are the building blocks to becoming as good as you can be in golf. Build a plan with a timeline and bench marks to keep you on task as you improve. Draw a timeline for one year with your handicap objectives on the upper side and the means to accomplish the objectives below it. A year's overview plan to move from a 15 to a 10 to a five handicap might look like this:

	15 handicap	10 handicap	5 handicap
January			
February			
March			
April			
May			
June			
July			
August			
September			
October			
November			
December			

Your detailed plan for one month might look like this one for June:

- Schedule and take two lessons from the pro.
- Videotape my swing at the beginning and then at the end of the month to note improvement.
- Practice 4 times a week for at least one hour. Practice my full swing for two thirds of the time and my short game for one third this month.
- Read: *Golf Digest, Golf Magazine,* and *Golf My Way,* by Jack Nicklaus.
- Play twice a week. Enter the city championship tournament.
- Record and track all my statistics and compare them with my previous months' statistics.
- Visit the gym three times a week for strengthening and flexibility work. Stress abdomen work this month.
- Get weight to 185 by the end of the month.

Such a sample month should suggest the kind of objectives you can set yourself in order to reach your goal. You may want to write your monthly plan at the beginning of each month rather than at the beginning of the year so you can make better adjustments depending on your progress and set your priorities according to your needs. This is much like a business plan to ensure that you cover all aspects of your improvement program and give attention where it is needed. You need to be flexible in your planning in order to make the gains needed by recognizing how to allocate your time and activity based on what is needed.

You need to track and keep both statistical data and anecdotal records of how you are progressing toward your goal. You can do this in a diary or with a computerized program. A good web site to see what such a program looks like is www.GolfDoctorStats.com. This type of program analyzes your game from many angles and offers commentary on your improvement, along with charts and graphs to help you analyze your game in depth. This is a much easier way than diary keeping to get statistics on such things as fairways hit in regulation, greens hit in regulation, number of putts, sand saves, up-and-downs, and weather. These programs range from simple to advanced, so shop around and select one that matches your needs and goal. They are well worth the low price and are vital to point out weaknesses and help you plan practice sessions accordingly.

In addition to the statistical part of the game, you must also track your affective realm, physical and mental preparation, and psychomotor connections. Some programs allow you to enter anecdotal records, but generally these anecdotal aspects are better suited to entries in a day book or journal of what you did during a particular round. You should note such things as the following:

Emotional well-being. Did you stay in the moment? Did you allow anger or frustration to affect your play? Did you avoid becoming too high (euphoric) or too low (discouraged)? How was your concentration and focus?

Mental preparedness. Did you have a game plan? Did you test the greens and sand before playing? Did you bring the correct configuration of clubs for the course? Did you ask about trouble areas on the course?

Nutrition. Did you eat properly the night before playing? Did you maintain good nutrition on the course? Did you stay hydrated?

Physical well-being. Did you stretch before and after playing? Was any muscle group feeling weak or painful? Did you warm up properly?

On-course management. Did you follow your game plan? Did you hew to your pre-shot routine? Did you read greens from the best routine? Did you make good shot and club selection decisions?

Such anecdotal records may be as important as the statistical analysis of your shot performance, if not more so, as they directly relate to the causes of the performance rather than just the results. Be very honest in your anecdotal recording. This part of your analysis is only for you and to improve and get where you want to be you have to know exactly what you are doing correctly and what you might be doing wrong. For example, if you omitted your pre-shot routine on the last five holes, make sure that you write this down. When you analyze your score, you might find that your play dropped off at the end and the lack of a pre-shot routine may explain why this happened.

Look for patterns in your statistics and anecdotal records. If you consistently fail to finish a good round and you mess up the last few holes, run through your records and see what might be happening. Were you getting tired? Had you forgotten to eat healthy snacks during the round? Did you forget to keep drinking water? Did you feel nervous about posting a good round instead of playing one shot at a time? Did you get out of your routine? Did something or someone make you angry or frustrated? You need to know these things in order to correct them. The act of writing them down and seeing them on paper or on a screen in front of you is a powerful tool to stregthen your commitment to getting better at golf. If you simply play and forget what happened, whether it was good or bad, you are throwing away data that should be in your mind as building blocks, not distant memories. This is what taking your game seriously means and it is part of the commitment to becoming the golfer that you want to become. The mere fact that you are devoting the time to sharpening your mind and gaining a true awareness of what happens to you on the golf course separates you from the average golfer.

I wrote this book after thinking about and observing golfers at all levels and watching how they sought to become better at the game. No one ever really masters the game. We have periods of greatness and we all are humbled by its complexity. My intention has been to make a road map of a route to becoming a better golfer in a systematic way, one that is based on the principles of learning and an understanding of how our minds operate. I sincerely hope that this book has brought some enlightenment, helps you become a better player, and makes the wonderful game of golf more enjoyable for you. I always look forward to getting feedback from my students and I look forward to hearing how well you are doing.

William C. Kroen Ph.D., LMHC
USGTF golf professional

Glossary

Address—the position taken as a player is ready to begin the swing.

Alignment—the setting of the body in relation to the intended target line.

Approach shot—a shot that is made toward the green.

Apron—the closely mown grass that surrounds a green.

Backswing—the moving of the club from the ball to the top or a paused position that occurs before the downswing.

Best ball—two players compete as a team. The lower of the two partners' scores is their team score.

Blade irons—clubs that have a thin top line and sole or bottom. Usually forged.

Blind shot—a shot taken where the pin or target cannot be seen.

Bounce—the angle of the sole of an iron, usually given in degrees. A sand wedge typically would have a bounce of 10 degrees front to back.

Bump and run—a shot that is hit low so that it lands on the fairway and bounces and rolls onto the green.

Bunker—a hollowed-out area on the course that is often filled with sand and designated as a hazard.

Butt—the end of the shaft where the grip is installed.

Carry—the distance the ball flies in the air from impact to the point where it lands.

Cast—clubs made from a casting mold. Cast clubs are usually made to create weighting properties to help make the clubs easier to hit.

Casting—letting go of the club at the top of the swing instead of holding the wrists in a cocked position when starting the downswing.

Choke down—placing the hands lower or toward the shaft on the grip.

Clutch—playing a great shot or playing well under pressure.

Divot—a patch of turf cut out by the club entering the ground.

Draw—a shot that is designed to curve from right to left.

Face—the front part of the club that comes in contact with the ball.

Fade—a shot that is designed to curve from left to right.

Fairway—the closely mown part of the course.

Fat—a shot in which the club strikes the ground behind the ball.

Flange—the base of a sand wedge that is wide to prevent digging into the sand too deeply.

Flat—a swing that moves around the torso rather than on a more upright path that brings the club over the shoulders.

Flex—the amount of stiffness of a shaft. In general, the basic shaft flexes are L (Ladies), A (Seniors), R (Regular), S (Stiff), X (Extra Stiff).

Follow-through—the completion of the forward swing; the finish.

Fried egg—a lie in a sand bunker in which the ball sits in a depression surrounded by a small ridge of sand.

Grain—the direction in which the grass grows.

Handicap—a number that a player uses to indicate his playing ability. It is used to equalize matches.

Heel—the part of the club face near the shaft.

Hook—a ball that flies wildly from right to left.

Hosel—the neck of the club; the part where club head and shaft are joined.

Lag—to hit a putt that will stop near the hole for an easy putt.

Launch angle—the angle in which the ball leaves the face of the club at impact.

Lie—where the ball comes to rest on the ground.

Lip—the rim of the hole.

Loft—the angle of the club face that produces lift to the shot.

National Golf Foundation—an organization that conducts statistical studies in many areas of the game of golf, including tracking trends.

Perimeter weighting—a weight distribution pattern in which weight is placed largely around the outer edges of the club face.

PGA Tour—the Professional Golfers Association tournament tour.

Pin—the flagstick.

Pitch—a short, high shot that lands and stops quickly.

Pull—a shot that flies to the left sharply.

Push—a shot that flies to the right sharply.

Rough—the heavy grass that borders a fairway.

Rules of Golf—compiled by the United States Golf Association and the Royal and Ancient Golf Club of St. Andrews, Scotland. Governs all play around the world.

Shaft—the long part of the club that connects the grip to the club head.

Shank—a shot in which the ball is struck on the hosel and flies wildly to the right.

Skull—a shot that strikes the ball near its equator.

Slice—a shot that flies wildly from left to right.

Sole—the part of the club that touches the ground; the bottom of the club head.

Stance—the position of the feet at address.

Statics—term used by Jack Nicklaus to define the steps that are made before a swing is made.

Take-away—the start of the backswing.